Life Aboard The Monkey Bus

James E. Martin

by

James E. Martin

Bloomington, IN Milton Keynes, UK

authorHOUSE

AuthorHouse™
1663 Liberty Drive, Suite 200
Bloomington, IN 47403
www.authorhouse.com
Phone: 1-800-839-8640

AuthorHouse™ *UK Ltd.*
500 Avebury Boulevard
Central Milton Keynes, MK9 2BE
www.authorhouse.co.uk
Phone: 08001974150

First published by AuthorHouse 10/12/2006

ISBN: 1-4259-5364-6 (sc)

Printed in the United States of America
Bloomington, Indiana
This book is printed on acid-free paper.

Library of Congress Control Number: 2006931978

Dedication

This book is dedicated to my Family and Friends who have encouraged me to write, all who have honored me through the purchase and reading of my previous books, the thousands of Children and their Teachers to whom I have read, and the hosts of Librarians having found merit in my work.

JAMES E. MARTIN

Contents

Life Aboard the Monkey Bus

On February 14, 1943, my U.S. Army Unit arrived at Salinas, Ecuador, South America, an Early Warning Station for the Panama Canal Defense Command. 2:00 a.m., while still at sea, an earthquake devastated Ecuador and there was fear of a tidal wave. Fortunately for us and the Ecuadorians, the tidal wave did not happen. Salinas is a fishing village located near the end of an arid peninsula approximately eight feet above sealevel extending seventeen miles East to the town of Liberatad at the foot of the Andes Mountains.

The bay of Salinas was too shallow to harbor even small ships, so it was necessary for the USS Johnson to anchor approximately three miles at sea. Men and freight were loaded upon barges, which were towed to shore by tug boats. The only tall building in the village was a shabbily constructed cathedral made of wood and painted red. A hotel, a restaurant, and a small one-story flat-roofed brick bank building were the only other substantial structures in the village. Most of the other business area buildings were made of adobe. All residences were squalled shacks made of drift-wood, crates, and sheets of tin. The only paved street was the main road inside the Army Camp. Since rain fell on average once every four years, the sand roads throughout Salinas and to Liberatad were sufficient for the burro traffic and the few light trucks being used. The earthquake caused only minor damage at Salinas.

Most of my fellow soldiers and I were fresh out of 'boot camp' and had never had any leave time, so after approximately three months at our new station, two of my friends and I were granted a three-day pass to Guayaquil, the nation's second largest city and only major harbor approximately ninety miles south of Salinas. We made the short flight to Guayaquil aboard a Pan-American Grace Lines plane and landed at the municipal airport surrounded by dense jungles several miles from the city. Heavy damage to poorly constructed buildings was evident everywhere along the route into the city. We soldiers, therefore, were glad that we had confirmed reservations at the Roxy Hotel.

At this time, I make it perfectly clear that living through an earth-quake could not have been more frightening than was our wild high-speed taxi ride with a maniac cab driver from the airport to our hotel. I have been told that when faced with almost certain death, a person's entire life experience passes before his eyes. That may be true, but what I was experiencing at that moment was the raw terror of being hurled through the Ecuadorian jungle like a human cannon-ball in contemplation of a short life. I could not believe that I was paying good money for that. That driver could have fully qualified as a Japanese Kamikaze pilot.

We soldiers did not know ten words of Spanish between us, but that driver must have understood our pronunciation of Guayaquil, because he immediately launched that missile in which we sat and randomly aimed it toward the city in a tire-squalling roar. With one hand casually resting upon the steering wheel and the other firmly pressing upon the horn button, he seemed to approach the speed of mach-1 within the first quarter mile. I felt as though I was riding inside a concrete mixer as he zigzagged through, around, and past crowds of pedestrians, bicyclists, and pony carts so unfortunate to be in his path. We spent as much time swooping through one side-ditch and then the other as we did on the pavement while that horn-blowing crackpot set out to establish a new land speed record. He clashed through the gears, his right foot pressing the accelerator to the floor, while leaving those hapless creatures behind us in an acute state of bewilderment. I am certain that he applied all aspects of the science of inertia and propulsion as he charted our immediate, but uncertain, future. As I observed those poor wretches dashing for their lives, I thought that, should I survive that ordeal, I probably should write my will.

Upon arriving upon city streets, we assumed that that madman would reduce speed and honor some established urban limit, but oh no. To our dismay, we began meeting increased numbers of his fellow drivers whom it was obvious had graduated from the same demolition driving school that our man did. Fear for my life quadrupled when I observed that none of the intersections were equipped with traffic control lights. It became clear that whomever blew his horn first had the right-of-way. The flaw with that idea was that all drivers were blowing their horns at the same time. In fact, our driver had not ceased blowing his horn the entire trip. Now the entire city was filled with a merry concert of beeping horns. A trip through a busy street intersection was a nail-biting nightmare. The drivers' adeptness at avoiding street corner collisions was a miracle that would evoke the ever-lasting admiration of a NASCAR driver.

For the poor pedestrians, it was an entirely different equation, however. I observed clusters of them at each busy crossing looking like sprinters crouched in starting blocks waiting to hear the pistol shot. Only the brave dared to play that game. With the slightest break in vehicular traffic, dozens would make the death-defying sprint to the other side. Many were missed by only inches from passing cars. Cars slowed only enough to avoid a last second collision with another vehicle. Pedestrians appeared to be of no concern to them.

I was practicing my new-found nail-biting past-time as we rocketed past the Roxy Hotel. I had already observed a gaggle of people leave the curb at the next street corner while we were in mid-block. The people were running for their lives to avoid being clobbered by our cab, when I clapped our driver on his back and shouted "Roxy!"

Main Street, Salinas, Ecuador

We were astonished when he zoomed through the intersection, took advantage of the wide street, made a tire-bawling U-turn on two wheels, and returned through the intersection terrorizing the same pedestrians whom he had narrowly missed as he now approached them from the opposite direction.

I could feel that my normally healthy condition had grown frail as he skidded to a stop before our hotel. I stood on weak trembling legs waiting for our baggage to be unloaded. That cab driver was one person I hoped to never see again.

The taxi ride dominated our conversation throughout dinner, but our attention was soon captured as a colorfully costumed band began playing lively Latin music. Dancers crowded the ballroom performing rumbas, sambas, and congas. Not in my dreams did this green-horn West Virginia farm-boy think that he would witness anything so exciting. We watched the dancing until the ballroom closed at 2: a.m.

Soldiers traditionally awaken at 5: a.m. With the hours of our short vacation rapidly ticking away, we didn't want to waste a second. We ate early breakfast at the hotel and exited the front door into the bright tropical sunlight. Near the equator, the length of daylight and darkness are exactly the same every day of the year. We planned a walking tour of the city and the weather that day was delightful. The sidewalks were already crowded and the car horns were beeping merrily. Now we, too, could engage in the street corner Russian-roulette sprint game with the natives.

One situation upon exiting the hotel caused us much amusement. No doubt many other American servicemen had visited Roxy Hotel before we did. Every young boy in Guayaquil must have been waiting outside hoping that some GIs would appear. The youths had learned that soldiers liked to wear well shined shoes, so everyone of them carried a shoeshine kit. Dozens swarmed around us the instant we stepped upon the sidewalk. All were shouting, "Shoe shine, Joe?" "Hey Joe, shoe shine uno cigareo, no mas." ("Only one cigarette.") "Shoe shine, veinte sinco centavos." (Twenty five cents.")

Those boys were determined businessmen who would not take "no" for an answer. They hopped, whooped, and tugged at our sleeves. By sheer force of numbers, they herded us to a nearby low stone wall surrounding a large monument where we were invited to sit. Among the three of us, of course, we had six shoes. One boy shined one shoe each; two boys for each man. That scheme yielded either two cigarettes or fifty centavos. Although they were competitors, the boys were polite and friendly with each other. Those who were not shining shoes stood patiently by until the job was almost done, at which time they scampered in mass to await our arrival at the next block, where they would gang around us again. They became such a nuisance, we approached two very stern looking policemen on patrol with ground length sabers strapped to their belts. We motioned that we wished to be left alone, so with a few harsh words spoken to the boys, they scattered in all directions not to be seen again until the following morning.

We spent the entire daylight hours visiting the museums, churches, statues, ornate government buildings and the harbor. Being from West Virginia Highlands, my greatest interest were the sights, sounds, smells, and activities of the busy harbor and ships flying flags of many nations. I was so fascinated by that strange environment, my friends had to drag me away. It became obvious to me that three days was much too short a time for me to see all that I wanted to see.

I was somewhat astonished that the natives, in general, were mostly non- conversant and hardly showed any curiosity towards us. Those who worked in places of business did not exhibit much salesmanship or merchandising approach to customers. Perhaps they were reticent because of the language barrier between us. They actually spoke very little among themselves. Most appeared to be Indians of small stature with black hair, dark skin, and dark eyes.

We arose again the morning of our second day, which we wished to spend touring the countryside. Arrangements were made with the hotel manager to hire a taxi driver with a reputation as a safe driver for us, who would be willing to spend the entire day showing us places of interest. He arrived early and we fed him breakfast at the hotel. We also had the hotel manager pack food and beverage enough to feed the four of us all day. With the aid of the driver, we pushed our way through the throng of shoeshine boys to reach our cab, surprisingly a modern Chrysler sedan. We hoped to travel many miles north of the city in hopes of gaining a glimpse of Chimborazo,

Ecuador's highest peak, but travel following the earthquake was inhibited by destroyed bridges and much fallen timber. We viewed many peaks of the Andes and saw many villages where residents were using primitive tools and methods of restoring their damaged homes and businesses.

We passed one small sawmill in operation. Having grown to adulthood with a West Virginia family engaged in the timber industry, I was interested to observe that operation in Ecuador. I was accustomed to the heavy Appalachian hardwoods, so when I observed a small slender Indian walk to a stack of logs and place one at least one foot in diameter and approximately twelve feet long upon his shoulder without any effort, I was so amazed. I had to try that for myself. We, in our foreign uniforms and traveling through a jungle region in a fancy car by Ecuadorian standards, had already created curiosity among the laborers, so they were puzzled as to why was I disturbing their log pile? To my amazement, I, too, could lift a similar log with little effort. That was when I discovered that the logs were balsa wood. I had been seeing giant trees throughout the day with huge trunks which appeared to be white-washed up to ten feet above the ground and whose canopies were enormous. The taxi driver, who had a vocabulary of a few English words, told us that the giant trees were balsa. Some of them were more than fifteen feet wide at their base.

Our day in the country was truly pleasant, but all vacations must come to an end, so on the morning of day three, we prepared to return to our base at Salinas. My two friends had bought round-trip plane tickets, so we parted after eating breakfast and paying our hotel bills. I wished to experience as much adventure as could be had in three days in that strange land where within its boundaries on any given day it is possible to experience spring, summer, fall, and winter. For that reason, I followed my plan to return to Salinas by train.

I was traveling with light luggage. The hotel manager told me that it was only a short walk to the depot. I had not traveled by train in Ecuador and did not know what to expect. I anticipated that there may be some delay because of recent earthquake damage. I could not take a chance of being late returning to my Army Unit.

*My friends and I (center) at base of a
Balsa tree, Guayaquil Ecuador 1943*

I had not traveled extensively back in the United States, but I had an idea of how a train station should look. I was not prepared for what I saw upon arriving at that one. It had open sides and a thatched roof made of palm branches supported by poles. It had a dirt floor and few crude benches were randomly scattered within its narrow rectangular space.

A crowd was waiting within, so I assumed that, this being Ecuador's second largest city, the station must be the boarding location for a variety of destinations. Women and children outnumbered men Infants were being carried papoose fashion inside narrow wicker baskets strapped to the mothers' backs. Although all sides of the station were open to outside air, stench in the place was almost unbearable for me. Much of the odor was attributable to numerous crates of half-decayed fruits and vegetables, in addition to cages of live pigs, chickens, ducks, and other creatures awaiting shipment. Worrisome thoughts entered my mind as I wondered if taking the train was a mistake. I was wanting adventure and it appeared that this trip may be an unforgettable one. There was no ticket counter, just a Station Agent roaming among the crowd gathering a hand full of Ecuadorian Sucres and stuffing them into his pockets.

Upon referring to my Spanish phrase booklet, I asked him, "Donda est el tren pora Salinas?"

With the wave of a hand, he gestured toward the railroad track.

I could not speak to the natives, because I did not know their language. The people did very little talking to each other. They did not seem overjoyed about making their trips. A sudden torrent of rain began to leak through that thatched roof. I couldn't see much more advantage of standing under the roof than merely standing in the rain. Judging from the unsanitary conditions of that place, it didn't take long for me to decide that I didn't want something washing through that thatch and falling on my skin. I walked to track side to take my first look at the roadbed.

What I saw was not reassuring. The rail bed consisted of a narrow-gage contraption of the most flimsy little steel rails that I had seen. They were reminded me of the light-weight tracks used inside coal mines in my native state of West Virginia. It would be unthinkable to entrust passenger safety to such flimsy road beds in any industrialized nation of the World. Those tracks made a wavy snake-trail pattern as far as I could see through the rain and fog. If I had enough money at that moment, I would have hired a taxi to return me to Salinas, but I had spent most of my money, having saved only enough to buy the train ticket.

My surprises for the day were only beginning. Instead of seeing a steam engine pulling cars into the station, a short dilapidated old yellow school bus mounted upon train wheels appeared through the fog. I looked with disbelief at the Station Agent. He grinned widely and gestured toward that apparition from another planet and shouted, "El tren pora Salinas." I looked helplessly back at that bus upon whose side was a poorly lettered sign which spelled 'autocariel', a Spanish name given such a contraption. Hoping that I was only having a bad dream, I forlornly looked once more at the station agent. "Salinas," he repeated.

Due to my reluctance to board the bus, I got the only remaining seat, which was in the second row in front of the animal crates stored behind the passenger seats. My seat-mate sitting next to the window was a woman with a papoose which smelled badly spoiled strapped to her back. Fortunately for me, she shifted the baby away from me between herself and the window.

I had observed a tall Indian wearing a 'gaucho' hat carrying a long-tailed monkey upon his shoulder, when I was briefly inside the station. That irritable monkey had been making a nuisance of itself, chattering like a magpie, and swiping claws at anyone who came near its master. Well, what do you know? That monkey and its master were now my close neighbors on the bus. They were occupying the seat directly behind me just in front of the animal crates. Maybe I did get some cooties in my hair while standing beneath that dripping roof, because the instant I took my seat, that monkey began picking what I hoped were imaginary lice off my scalp. When it wasn't play-ing pinochle on my head, it was resting both of its front feet upon the back of my seat, thrusting its head between myself and the papoose woman, craning its neck around my shoulder, looking directly at my face, grinning widely, and showing its filthy yellow teeth. It suddenly snatched my uniform cap which I had tucked beneath the shoulder epaulet of my shirt. He recoiled back upon its master's shoulder and jammed my cap Barney Fife fashion down upon its head forcing its ears forward.

That was when my tolerant good nature came to an end. I turned about facing that pair with a savage snarl on my face, demanding that the man recover my cap and return it to me. The monkey took ref-uge atop a filthy pig crate where he removed my cap and sat upon it and would not permit the Indian to have it. When they struggled, the defiant monkey stuffed my cap between the slats of the crate where it fell into the filthy goop below. The Indian also lost his patience with the monkey, grasped it by the scruff of its neck, and held it at arms' length, while he retrieved my cap. He sheepishly handed it to me. I was furious as I snatched the dripping cap from his hand. A cap is a required part of the Army uniform, but I was not about to place that filthy thing upon my head. I encased it inside a couple of my soiled socks and crammed into my satchel. During that entire fracas, the Indian woman sharing my seat stared placidly ahead as though nothing was happening.

The autocariel did not depart the station immediately as time was allowed to load additional crates of squealing pigs, assorted poultry, and vegetables in the remaining storage space. With the loading of our barnyard travel companions completed, the train began to move. My body began to sense a gravel-sifter sort of side to side motion as the old bus began a belly-dancing rhythm as it gained speed along that wavy track. I found myself praying out loud for deliverance as I suddenly remembered that scary trip two days earlier with that maniac taxi driver from the airport to the hotel. That was one adventure which I did not want to repeat. Now here I was confined inside a refugee from a junk yard, surrounded by people I couldn't talk to, and sharing breathing space with a gaggle of chickens, pigs, a monkey, and an unsanitary papoose. I ask, is that adventure or what?

For the present, I was focused upon that slovenly mannered conductor who was a picture of relaxation. He looked as though he was feeling the symptoms of an on coming early morning nap. My prayer intensified as I wondered how that man could effectively apply brakes to that monstrosity with four steel wheels running upon wet steel tracks. How would that rocking vehicle hold sharp curves on steep mountain grades? And why were those two Indians lying face down and rearward upon each of the running boards in the rain? Why were they each holding a sugar scoop? What were those open-topped boxes of sand for?

The rain continued to pour in jungle proportions and my questions were soon answered in rushing short order, when we approached the first down grade. The instant the nose of the bus dipped below the crest of the hill, it sprang into new life and quickly gained speed down that wavy track. The conductor also sprang into action as he grasped a spinner knob attached to the rim of the steering wheel. He vigorously spun the wheel until it could go no further, because lengths of chain were welded to the steering wheel shaft in such a manner that they would wind around it. The ends of the chains were attached to levers which activated the brakes. The Indians lying upon the running boards were busy scooping sand from the boxes upon the rails. The wheels must have been locked into a complete skid, since they were emitting a high-pitched ear-splitting screech. The problem was, the bus was not slowing. I really needed to return to the top of that hill to retrieve my heart, which had leaped from my body in fear. Now, I realized why nobody was smiling, including myself.

Why was I ever so foolish as to yearn for adventure? At that moment, I wished that I was any place other on earth. I was riding a tiger's back. I didn't want to stay on, but I couldn't get off. I was really impressed by our chances of survival, when I saw some of the women counting rosary beads. I took hope from the fact that most of the passengers were much older than I and I reasoned that they must have survived that trip many times. It became obvious the reason they were not speaking to each other was because they were in deep meditation with their Maker. Even the monkey was leaving my head lice alone.

Along the seventy miles from Guayaquil to Liberatad, there were many steep grades. Feeling as a person playing Russian Roulette at the top of each incline, I helplessly accepted my destiny and trusted whatever providence which had protected me thus far. The frantic action of the three-man crew was repeated each time we reached a down-grade, but hills go both ways. Those which we had to climb were often as steep as those we had to descend. The bus crept at a crawl on most of them, but sometimes, the wheels spun to a complete stop. At those times, a device attached to the rear of the bus that could be activated remotely and dropped into place by the conductor from his driving position prevented the vehicle from running backwards completely out of control. The thought of that happening caused my adenoids to ache. When stalls happened, all of the male passengers would dismount and push until forward progress resumed. We didn't have to sprint to catch up and remount. What I did not see was any pig or monkey power being used.

The pleasant adventure I hoped to experience came during more relaxing moments when viewing the magnificent scenery and many quaint jungle villages where passengers got off and others boarded. At one such station, the man with the monkey departed. At another, the woman sharing my seat also left. At each stop, more animals and other freight were loaded and unloaded. Since the railroad consisted of only a single track, it was at those villages where side-tracks existed, thus eliminating the probability of head-on collisions. It was also at those villages where I saw clones of that bus I was riding. I marveled that there was more than one like it. What a market that country could have been for discarded street cars from more advanced nations.

Stops at those village stations usually lasted approximately ten minutes. The rain had stopped. With the arrival of tropical sunshine coupled with the departure of the monkey and that fragrant papoose, my mood improved considerably. Without allowing myself to become foolhardy, I began to think that I was beginning to 'get the hang' of that autocariel riding.

My optimism was short lived, however, for it wasn't long after leaving the last village pig stop before reaching Lieberatad the bus arrived at the crest of the longest hill I had seen during the trip. The road bed ran straight for approximately two miles. It had a steep beginning and gradually leveled at the bottom much like a ski jump. I felt prayers creeping back into my mentality, but the huge gulp competing with words in my throat prevented me from praying out loud. That bus took off like a rocket sled. The wheels were screaming so shrilly that I had to plug my ears with my fingers. I was sitting by the window now, where I could plainly see the 'sand Indian' in action on my side of the bus. The air movement was so swift that every scoop of sand he intended to pour under the skidding wheel simply blew away. The vehicle must have been traveling sixty miles per hour and the conductor was incapable of slowing its progress. I began to understand why jungle babies began to smell spoiled, when almost a mile ahead, I saw five cows standing upon the railroad track. It was obvious the conductor was scared. The bus was not slowing a bit. The only thing remaining to do was to sound the bus's feeble horn. Even that monkey could have made more noise than that horn did. It sounded like the muffled bellow of a moose. That was one situation which left no doubt of 'where's the beef?' I had visions of chipped beef from the front, pork fricassee from the rear, with me filling in the middle. I was going to be a crash dummy entrapped inside a decrepit trash dumpster on wheels and there was nothing I could do about it. Closer we came. I had been around cattle most of my life and was able to read some of their intentions when they were about to react. Perhaps it was the screeching of the wheels that first captured their attention. Cows have poor ability to focus upon moving things, especially at a distance, but I had my first flicker of hope while we were still half a mile away from creating Hamburger International. The cows turned facing the bus, perked their ears forward, and held their heads high. Just when the cow catcher mounted upon the front of that bus was about to serve its designed purpose, the cows raised their tails above their backs and galloped into the jungle. Whe-e-w! The pause which spells relief.

I do not think it is necessary to explain to you the weakened condition of my health upon leaving that autocariel, but I will do it anyway. Also, when I boarded a US Army bus at Liberatad, my clothing wet, disheveled, and reeking with assorted barnyard odors, I was not surprised that the other soldiers would not take seats near me. Then there was the Military Police gate guard at the Post Main Gate at Salinas. He did not even try to understand why I was not wearing my uniform cap. He also was not favorably impressed by my rumpled soaked uniform. And where were those shoe-shine boys when I truly needed them? To make that story short, that MP wrote me a citation which definitely was not a love letter for me to deliver to my First Sergeant. My kind leader quickly realized that, after an ordeal such as I had endured, I plainly needed a rest from my ordinary duties, so he sentenced me to a week of KP (kitchen police) washing pots and pans under the tender care of a most unfriendly mess sergeant.

ADVENTURE? Bah humbug!

Nice Kitty

It is easy to imagine that everything associated with war is unpleasant, but that is not always true. There are times and places which are absolutely wonderful. A temporary respite from the drudgery of war and its inherent duty. I recall Christmas day of 1942, while in basic training at Fort Clayton, Panama Canal Zone, my Unit was taken on tour of the ruins of the original Panama City on the Pacific Ocean side of the Canal. We visited the Saint Anastasius Church, built in 1537, it is the oldest church in the Western Hemisphere. It was destroyed and left in ruins by the pirate Henry Morgan and his buccaneers during 1671. It was said to have an altar coated by pure gold. When the natives were warned that the pirates were raiding old Panama City, natives covered the altar with white-wash hoping that the gold would not discovered, but the ruse was not successful.

There was one break from our arduous training when we spent a week-end at Farfan Beach along the north side of the Canal. That was much like being back home, since families of American engineers and Canal employees who lived near-by in US Government housing also used the beach. Back at Fort Clayton, one of my fellow trainees captured a harmless tree iguana measuring over five feet in length. He carried it coiled in his hand like a rope until reaching the beach, where he mischievously swam with it far out in the water and released it. Similar to some Loch Ness sea monster, the iguana held its head high and skimmed across the water toward the shore. The sight of it caused screaming women and children to dash from the water, but when they saw that was a tree iguana like the ones which played on their lawns every day, they had a good laugh.

On one occasion, we relieved the stress of training and the yearning to be back home, when some of my friends and had a Sunday free from duty. We loaded our pockets with candy bars, cigarettes, Zippo lighters, small mirrors, and cigars purchased at the Post Exchange and broke regulations by hiking several miles on a jungle trail to see the native village of Reo Baju whose elephant grass huts were roofed by using palm branches. We relieved the suspicion which the natives may have had of us by presenting as gifts the items we had purchased. In return, the inhabitants treated us to a tour of the village. To me, it was like stepping back in time a thousand years.

My group graduated from sixteen weeks of basic training under the tender care of our drill master/house father, Sergeant Click. We were assigned to a combination Coast Artillery/Anti-aircraft Artillery Battalion at one of earth's true garden spots at ancient Fort Amador,

Ruins of oldest church in the Americas
built near Balboa, Panama 1537 AD

only a few miles from Fort Clayton. I fell in love with that beautiful place bounded on one side by the Canal where it empties into the Pacific Ocean and by the gorgeous city of Balboa on the other.

The safety of the Panama Canal and its locks was every soldier's mission. To increase that safety factor at each of the three lock complexes along the canal, thousands of barrage balloons near one fourth the size the Goodyear Blimp anchored to concrete bases and tethered approximately five hundred feet above ground by one inch thick steel cables stretched for miles in all directions on each side of the Canal. Hundreds of powerful search lights were located in the same areas occupied by the balloons. The balloons were installed to snarl and crash any enemy low-flying planes intending to destroy the locks. The central locks named Pedro Miguel are located inside a deep cut through a mountain. To discourage a plane from flying low above it, a steel mesh submarine net, usually used to secure harbors, was anchored to the mountain-top on each side of the locks and dangled above them just high enough to allow the tall masts of ships to pass beneath it.

Although our Battery headquarters was located at Fort Amador, we had an anti- aircraft gun position atop one mountain over-looking Pedro Miguel lock. Each platoon was rotated to two weeks duty at that position, where we had two forty millimeter anti-aircraft guns and two fifty caliber machine gun emplacements, one steel Quonset hut containing an orderly room and supply room, another Quonset hut used as a kitchen and dining room, and four canvas squad tents semi-permanently draped over two-by-four wooden frames attached to elevated wooden floors, which shielded us from snakes and the twice daily torrential rains. A small combination toilet and bath house completed the small camp. The camp proper was situated upon a flat shelf of the mountain with the weapons position located up a narrow jungle path leading to the mountain top. I also loved duty at that location, a jungle paradise where, at any hour day or night, one could gaze down upon huge ships passing through the lock. First Sergeant Poison, whose name belied his pleasant personality, assigned we soldiers from headquarters to our bi-weekly duty at Pedro Miguel, but a permanent party assigned there consisted of an administrative sergeant, a supply corporal, two cooks, and a mess sergeant. Individual

Officers were also assigned on a rotational basis each day as Officer of the Day. For that duty, each one commuted from Fort Amador to the out-post until our Battery was transferred to an 'early warning station' in South America during February 1943.

A typical day began with thirty minutes of physical exercise at five o'clock AM followed by breakfast. Shower, shaving and quarters cleaning followed breakfast. At nine, crew members not assigned kitchen police or night-time guard duty, climbed the mountain to engage in combat training and cleaning of weapons until eleven thirty. After lunch, due to the terrible heat, we took siesta until two. From two until four, we attended classes and watched training films. Each of we privates performed one day kitchen police and one night-guard duty each week during our two-week stay. Everyone was on twenty four alert in case of an air attack during our out-post assignment, so we were not permitted to go on pass.

This story is really about the out-post mess sergeant. He had a reputation of being a tyrant and his was the true essence of life imitating art. If he had a friend nobody knew it and the man seemed to hate everyone. Except when the necessity of duty required it, he did not associate with anyone. The fact was, he was a 'born-again alcoholic'. As soon as each evening meal had been served, he left the cooks in charge of having the kitchen cleaned. He walked down the steep road to where the paved road lead past the locks and toward Balboa and Panama City. There he would board a small bus called a 'cheva', the Panamanian word for goat. Chevas did not follow an established route, but would act like a taxi and deliver passengers where ever they wished to go. He always became drunk, but the Army's military police patrols would always start soldiers toward their units in time to get there before eleven o'clock curfew. Each night, Mess Sergeant could be heard puffing and grumbling his way back up the steep road just after curfew.

The single thing which upset the Mess Sergeant the most was untidiness around the trash and garbage collection area across the road from the mess-hall. All the men agreed that keeping the waste storage area clean and lids tightly closed atop the metal cans was important, because even you who have never lived in the tropics will readily understand how unpleasant decaying waste would smell if exposed to the heat of the tropical sun.

A neat little latticework enclosure had been built approximately thirty feet from the mess hall to contain the waste cans. The sergeant inspected that storage area several times each day, hoping to find carelessness on the part of some hapless kitchen policeman. Many a poor KP felt that his very soul had been singed by the tongue-lashing that mess sergeant could deal out. The sergeant was convinced that there was a conspiracy among the younger men to wait until he went to town each night and that they would deliberately upset garbage cans and scatter litter upon the ground. Night after night, the grouchy old sot would stagger up the trail to find most garbage cans upset. Pity the poor Kps on duty the following morning. He would have them out there practically mopping the earth attempting to eradicate the putrid odor.

Well, if any of you doubt that there is any meaningful justice in this world, take heart. This event happened one night during the dark phase of the moon. The sergeant was making his usual night-time climb up the hill, when from a short distance, he heard noise coming from the trash area. Mustering as much stealth as his condition would permit as he crept near, a body with head and shoulders submerged inside a can became dimly visible. When Sarge delivered a swift kick in the pants of the intruder, that jaguar ripped off the sergeant's shirt and left double claw marks from his shoulders to his belt-line.

There is little doubt that he set a new world record of getting sober. I was not there when his hospital stay was over, but I can attest to the tranquility which abounded during the final days of my last duty at that location.

A Day on Submarine Patrol

The only airplane ride taken during my first twenty years of life was the ninety mile flight from Salinas, Ecuador to Guayaquil. The year was 1943, when I was stationed at Salinas with the United States Army. My Unit had arrived there aboard the USS Johnson, a ratty old tub best described as a 'tramp steamer' hastily outfitted for war-time duty as a combination freight and troop transport, which was only seaworthy enough to operate in costal waters. It made monthly supply runs delivering food and clean bed linens from the Quartermaster Laundry at Corozal, and other freight from Panama to the Galapagos Islands, to Salinas, thence to Talara, Peru, and return to Balboa Harbor, Panama. On one voyage between Panama and the Galapagos Islands, it was sunk by a Japanese torpedo, our food supply lost, and we had to eat emergency rations of corned beef hash three meals per day for a month, before being re-supplied.

In addition to the Army, the United States Navy also maintained a bomber base of PBM Flying Boats at Salinas. Seeing those huge two-engine planes taking off and landing was a common daily sight beautiful to behold. They appeared from a distance to gracefully land as softly as would a swan. Once landing was complete, the pilots would taxi them across the bay to the shore. There, Navy divers would float a set of landing wheels beneath the plane and bolt them into place. A cable was hooked to the landing gear following which a winch would pull the plane out of the water onto a concrete ramp for safe storage, refueling, and reloading of explosive depth-charges for the next day's patrol.

The planes departed each morning just after first light and returned each night before dark. Their mission was to patrol the ocean in search of Japanese submarines. It was important that flying boats never attempt take-offs and landings during darkness, for should they strike a floating object, due to the great pressure of combined speed and weight in the water, even a bottle would rupture the hull and cause the plane to crash.

I had always dreamed of flying, but my concepts of doing so were by taking off and landing upon firm ground. I have always loved adventure, so when orders arrived directing our Unit to be transferred six hundred miles across the Pacific Ocean to the Galapagos Islands, I was anxious to go. It was into those flying boats that my comrades and I were loaded early one morning.

When ready, the winch operator eased the PBM into the water and the Navy divers once more entered the water to remove the landing wheels. My heart raced with excitement as I tried to adjust to the strange surroundings. I sat upon the floor strapped to the wall by a safety belt. Any idea I had that the take-off would be soft and smooth was a miscalculation. Even the slow taxi into the open bay was accompanied by the deafening noise of those powerful engines and the water sounded as though it was sloshing inside my head. The propellers blowing water against the outside of the plane's body sounded like a shower of rocks, much like sitting inside your car as it passes through a car-wash. I attempted look through the glass-covered portholes along each side of the plane, but the view was obliterated by flying spray.

The pilot, having reached a satisfactory take-off point, gunned the engines and the plane gathered speed. I truly thought my world was ending. Until that time I had never heard such deafening noise. I doubted that the bottom of that fuselage could withstand the turbu-lence of the water as it crashed into each wave on the water's surface. Amid all of the noise and confusion, I questioned the plane's abil-ity to lift off, but after what seemed forever, the noise of bashing waves gave way to the clear roar of the engines. By comparison, it almost seemed to be an eerie silence as the plane with its full load of fuel, depth charges, bombs, and a belly full of soldiers struggled to gain altitude. After the lapse of five minutes, the plane leveled at an altitude of approximately one thousand feet and the engines settled into a steady drone. The passing air cleared the water from the portholes and we had a clear view of the ocean now that we were free to wander about the plane. It would have been easy to see a submerged submarine in the clear water of the Pacific on such a sunny day. The plane spent the entire day zigzagging across a wide band of the ocean, while also gradually making forward progress, timing so as to cover the straight-line six hundred mile distance from Salinas to the Galapagos Islands before dark. Occasionally, we came into view of other PBMs, who were also participating in the submarine patrol.

Near five o'clock afternoon, a Navy crew-member appeared in the cock-pit doorway and instructed us to sit and refasten our safety belts. The pilot soon nosed the plane downward into a long gentle glide. For several minutes, the engines seemed to only whisper, but suddenly, the plane seemed to brake violently in mid-air as the wing-flaps were lowered and the engines were once more throttled to high power as they strained against the dragging effect of the flaps. Just as the plane was contacting the water, the pilot raised the nose slightly and cut the power almost entirely.

If I thought the take-off was a frightening experience, I was poorly prepared for the landing. When the belly of that plane touched the water, the sensation was like hitting a stone wall. Had my safety belt not been fastened, I would have hurtled through the plane's interior, out the windshield, and into the ocean. The noise was absolutely ear shattering, and the reverse gravity straining my body against the seat-belt lasted for at least a half mile before the plane came to a halt and quietly settled into the water. A great silence occurred and I was only vaguely aware of the gentle lapping of water against the fuselage.

We soldiers, unaccustomed to such an environment, stared at each other in silence, seeming to question had we just crashed or was this just everyday normal on a flying boat? Everybody began talking at once, happy to be alive, and commenting that the day had just been plain wild. Fortunately for the Japanese and German navies, we saw no enemy submarines that day.

The pilot re-throttled the engines and I could once more feel the shudder of the crashing waves. Soon the motors were silenced, the swimmers' voices could be heard as they attached the floating wheels, and the tug of the winch cable could be felt drawing the PBM up the inclined ramp.

As darkness fell upon this strange land, we dismounted from trucks at our new home. A large crowd of friends whom we had known at boot-camp in Panama welcomed us. We were soon sitting around long tables inside a mess hall, eating supper, and excitedly talking about our trip. I couldn't help wondering, if I were fortunate enough to eventually return to our quiet little country village of Smoot, West Virginia, would I ever be able to make my family and farm neighbors believe some of the experiences I was having. Nah. I don't think so. They would just turn away and say, "That young 'whipper-snapper' is trying to fill us with hot air."

Three Sisters

This event happened during 1943 on a tiny island in the Pacific Ocean six hundred miles west of the nation of Ecuador, South America. I was stationed with the United States Army at what was called an 'early-warning station' on San Cristobal Island, one of fifteen in a group named Galapagos, which means Turtle in Spanish. They are also sometimes called the Archipelago of Colon. They were named after the huge amphibian turtles living there, some of which reach five hundred pounds in weight. The islands have also been known as 'The Enchanted Isles', because pirates used them to bury stolen treasure. Mutineers and other castaways were abandoned there to die. Robinson Caruso (Alexander Selkirk) once visited the islands. Charles Darwin, the Author of Origin Of The Species, explored the islands during 1832 and was, no doubt, influenced by what he saw there in formulating his Theory Of Evolution. Later still, Author Zane Grey explored Galapagos, following which he wrote of wonderful adventures in his interesting book titled 'Tales Of Fishing In Virgin Seas.'

Prior to World War II, the government of Ecuador maintained San Cristobal as an exile prison camp. Due to the warm climate, housing was not provided them and the only food the prisoners had to eat was caught from the surrounding ocean. Since there was no liquid for them to drink, the Ecuadorian Government populated the island with thousands of goats in order that the prisoners could survive upon their milk. When the United States Government leased the island to establish the early warning station, consisting of a small Navy Base and Army Bomber/fighter base, the prisoners were gone, but the goats remained. They had no fear of man, so they were a nuisance who frequently invaded our barracks, mess halls, and made beds on the seats of our vehicles. They had no natural enemies, so they thrived upon our toothpaste, shaving cream, handkerchiefs, towels, wash-cloths, socks, underwear, sheets, and by raiding garbage cans. If someone was negligent enough to leave a barracks door ajar, it was not unusual to return from duty to find goats relaxing upon our bunks. They loved to occupy the seats of our trucks and jeeps. A more serious problem was, they were a perpetual runway hazard for departing and returning aircraft.

Strange birds and animals live at Galapagos, none of which have fear of man. They include a rare cormorant which cannot fly; penguins believed only to live in the Antarctic; and mocking birds of a type unknown elsewhere. Sea birds include herons and large goose-like boobies, gulls, and huge pelicans. Millions of lizards called iguanas, four feet in length and resembling hissing dragons, live throughout the islands.

The ocean surrounding the islands teamed with mammoth tuna, huge hammer-head sharks, electric eels, and manna-rays ten feet in diameter. They often rose above the water and would flap their wing-like bodies , slapping the water with such force upon re-entry, the resulting sound resembled that of a cannon firing. Both bird and ocean life was so competitive, it was an even chance of catching a bird or a fish the instant before the bait reached the water's surface. It was not unusual to catch an unwanted pelican with only a white rifle cleaning patch for bait.

All of the islands were formed by volcanic eruption, but only the one upon which our Army Base was located was flat enough to accommodate an air-base. All were arid with sparse vegetation consisting of cacti, cat-claw thorn bushes, salt grass, and a few other species of shrubs. In most aspects, that environment resembled a lava-covered moonscape. The islands could not support a population, so during my stay, there was none, except a colony of approximately thirty Norwegians who abandoned their homeland and was granted a charter by Ecuador to occupy the southernmost tip of the largest island, a small portion of which actually had rainfall and lush vegetation. It was at that colony eighty-five miles from our Base that the United States Navy filled barges with fresh water for us to drink.

Among my Unit's other duties of manning anti-aircraft and coast artillery guns, we were also in charge of two fifty foot open decked launches used as 'crash boats' to rescue pilots of P-39 fighter and B-24 bomber planes belonging to the Army Air Corps, should they crash at sea. Since there were no towns to visit for recreation, we soldiers entertained ourselves by swimming, fishing, having beach cook-outs, and by exploring the other islands. There were numerous small islands as well as thousands of submerged volcano craters surrounding the larger islands just a few feet below water surface. To prevent we soldiers from going crazy from loneliness, our Commander allowed us to use one of the off-alert crash boats to sail around the major islands for recreation as well as to watch for possible Japanese invaders, who may intend to launch a sneak-attack upon the Panama Canal. To guard against such a surprise, usually thirty or forty well-armed men went on those exploration trips.

The equator passes through the Galapagos Islands which were perpetually locked into an equatorial-high weather pattern. The sun shined every day, skies were always clear, and it never rained in the Galapagos, except where the Norwegian colony was located. There were no storms nor wind. Every day was just like every other day. The only turbulence near the shores were the two daily ocean tides.

During the forenoon of the day about which this story is written, we were cruising along and fishing while Sergeant Webb, who was a Maine fishing boat captain in civilian life, piloted our boat. We were skirting the Eastern coast of the largest island at a distance of approximately fifty miles from our Base, when near the horizon, we came into view of three small peaks crowded together. From that distance, they appeared to be tiny, but upon drawing near, we could plainly see that they were three volcanoes approximately five hundred feet in height rising from the sea.

Circling around three sides of the small peninsula jutting from the large island where the three stood, their bases almost touching each other, we were staring at vertical walls near twenty feet high. All the while, within ten to twenty feet of the water's surface, we were looking down into dozens open craters of miniature dormant volcanoes resembling aquariums teaming with the feeding frenzy of species too numerous to list. The violent scene was almost unnerving to behold as the mighty ate the weak.

We did not find any easier access than the twenty foot wall along the base of the volcanoes, but upon ending our search, we came upon a tiny inlet approximately two hundred feet wide with a most beautiful sandy beach. We were instantly startled as we awakened a colony of nearly one hundred sea-lions, some of whom ranged in weight from baby pups to old bulls weighing nearly five hundred pounds. When the bow of our boat passed the entry of that cove, pandemonium erupted as the sea-lions bellowed with alarm and lumbered into the water . They instantly becalmed themselves in the water and became curious about we strange intruders into their private world. We had previous encounters with sea-lions and discovered that they acted like pets begging for food. They especially like oranges. We always carried an assortment of food upon those explorations, so the sea-lions surrounding our boat were soon eating from our hands.

We had noticed that one of the volcanoes appeared to have a roof, so we chose to climb it. Fearing for the boat's safety as well as ours, Sergeant Web was uncomfortable about lingering near the rough cliffs any longer than necessary. Except for taking along necessary scaling equipment, we left all unnecessary equipment aboard the boat. We began using ropes to scale the sea-side wall. When we were safely ashore, Webb and the two men he selected to stay with himself and the boat, moved a couple hundred yards to sea and dropped anchor to await our return.

In the torrid heat, we began our climb. The angle of the volcano wall was approximately fifty degrees with loose volcanic ash so deep it neared the tops of our boots with each step. You may gain some idea of how difficult was our climb, if you imagine trying to climb a huge mound of wheat. There was nothing to which we could hold onto. Should anyone lose balance, he could possibly tumble into the ocean. For the sake of caution, teams of several men stationed themselves at intervals along a length of scaling ropes during the climb and upon the return. To add to our peril, at various times when we came near the nests of a small specie of eagle, the adult birds would assail us causing some painful scratches upon our skin and threatening our precarious balance on that steep surface.

After almost an hour of the most arduous climbing, we reached the summit. We definitely were not prepared for the surprises we found there. First, we worked our way around the wall of the volcano to view the other two others. When looking down to see how far apart the three were, we could not believe our eyes. At their shared base was a level field near the size of a baseball diamond. Someone had rolled stones of lava-rock near the size of office desks together to form the edges of a rectangle approximately two hundred by one hundred feet, resulting in what resembled a giant bill-board advertisement. Within its boundaries, having used smaller stones, was spelled 'Fiddlers Incorporated, London, England.'

Our initial amazement had scarcely abated when we had another surprise. I stated earlier that the peak which we had climbed appeared to be covered by a roof. Actually it did, appearing to have been the last large bubble of lava which had not completely burst from the force of the eruption. The roof was complete except for a small window-like opening on one side. One of our men who had a flashlight in his kit, shined it into the black interior of the volcano to see if he could see the bottom of the cone. When scanning the inside wall, the beam illuminated a small shelf of lava approximately fifteen feet down on one side of the bubble. Apparently to attract attention, a white handkerchief was impaled into the soft tacky lava wall by a sharp sliver of stone directly above an aluminum cigar box resting upon the shelf. Everyone was clamoring to know how the box happened to be there, so it was decided that a britches buoy would be made using a scaling rope into which a man would be lowered into the crater to get the box. I, being the smallest and lightest of the exploration party, was asked to volunteer to be lowered into that dark hole. Safely secured inside the rope seat, I was lowered to the level of the shelf. When I announced that I was in the appropriate position, I set myself into swinging, thus, allowing me to take the box from the shelf.

When I was safely outside, I was permitted to be the one opening the box. Perfectly preserved in that arid climate was a letter containing the logo of Fiddlers, Incorporated. It stated that Fiddlers was a British financial company who owned a racing yacht, that, during 1921 (the year of my birth) was engaged in an-around-the-world race. They, too, had observed the strange volcanic formation and had stopped there for a day of rest from the arduous work of manning sails. They left a request that should anyone also pass that way and discover their letter, to please write to tell what was the finder's purpose for visiting that remote spot.

We soldiers were prohibited from communicating our location to unauthorized persons during war-time censorship, so the best that we could do was enter our names and the date on the back side of the letter, explain how we happened to be there, and I was lowered inside once more to replace the box upon the shelf for some future traveler to find. Sixty three years later at the time of this writing, I still feel intrigued by that strange experience and can only wonder if the contents of that box has been found by someone else. By late afternoon, we signaled Sergeant Webb that we were ready to re-board the boat and return to Base elated by such a wonderful experience.

Daphne Major

It just stands there shaped like a soup bowl, looking black from a distance, arid, treeless, and jutting five hundred feet out of the Pacific Ocean. Even though the equator runs through it, the water surrounding its base is frigid to the touch, because it is bathed by the Humbolt Current flowing north a thousand miles from Antarctica. It receives no wind and no rain, because its atmosphere is locked into a perpetual equatorial high pressure system known as 'the doldrums.' That same condition existing is the Atlantic Ocean along South America's northern coast during the era of sailing ships bore the name 'horse latitudes', because Spanish ships carrying horses to the 'New World' were stalled for weeks with slackened sails. The crews were put to work rowing the ships with oars to make any forward progress and horses were thrown overboard to lighten the loads.

Most of the time, the ocean surface surrounding Daphne Major, is as smooth as a mirror. The influence of the daily high tides cause only gentle rolling swells, which scarcely produce breakers along the shoreline. Such is the apparent tranquility of life at Daphne Major, a dead volcano of approximately twenty square miles or less standing alone among the Galapagos Island group.

From our United States Army Base located on San Cristobal Island, which during World War II we called Little Seymore. Daphne Major and its nearest neighbor, Daphne Minor are in clear view eleven miles away from San Cristobal and separated from each other by approximately five miles. The two off-shore islands were as different as day and night. Instead of being cone shaped and almost perfectly round, Daphne Minor is a five hundred foot high vertical rectangular rock. Of course, the reason for their difference is locked into the mysterious geologic history of our planet's violent formative development. One can only assume that Daphne Minor was a solid core which plugged the violent eruption of a volcano, after which through weathering process, its soft volcanic ash washed away into the ocean. If that is true, how does one explain that happening in a region where rain never falls and wind does not blow?

The main purpose of my story is to focus upon the mysterious Daphne Major. It is a perfectly-shaped conventional volcano whose sloping sides are so steep that a person cannot stand erect when climbing it. One must touch the side with his hands just to maintain balance. Judging from the fact it is approximately eight or ten miles in circumference at the water's edge, its open crater at least a mile wide at its brim, and not knowing to what tremendous depth it must extend below the ocean, it is a huge volcano.

San Cristobal is approximately the same size, but it is flat, has a good harbor for the Navy Base, room for our artillery installation, and ample space for runways to accommodate the Army Air Corps heavy bombers and fighter craft.

Since soldiers must perform vigorous physical conditioning at all times, the level surface of San Cristobal did not offer much challenge for that purpose. Our Commanding officer saw Daphne Major as an instrument for both physical training as well as a site for practicing beach landings. So, in addition to frequent treks around San Cristobal carrying complete combat gear, we made an assault on Daphne Major. Embarking upon a new experience is always exciting as you know, but the prospect of exploring enchanting islands, which heretofore had been visited by only few people such as Morgan Morgan, Blue Beard, Charles Darwin, Alexander Selkirk (author of Robinson Caruso), and Zane Grey was a great thrill for me.

As we drew near, it was obvious that the black surface as seen from a distance was blotched by white bird guano, and the white feathers of tens of thousands of nesting sea-birds, a partial list including terns, gulls, pelicans, and large goose-like birds called boobies.

We had very little difficulty transferring ourselves and our equipment from our heavy wooden boats onto the steep shore as approximately two hundred scrambled onto the rocks, but that is where anything but easy began. You must understand that all creatures inhabiting the Galapagos Islands have not become acquainted with humans, so they have absolutely no fear of man. Being accustomed to competition with each other for space, where they sat is exactly where they were determined to stay. Anyone who invaded their space could expect to pay a painful price. It seemed laughable to think that tough combat soldiers could be repulsed by a concentration of birds, but from the first step from our boats, we were pecked, flopped, and buffeted by birds. The heavy boobies inflicted painful bites, which brought blood from exposed skin. Only our boots and canvas leggings protected our legs below our knees.

There was no vacant space upon which to step without crushing eggs and nestlings in various stages of development from those just hatched, to balls of fuzz, to near adult, in addition to grown birds refusing to budge an inch. Even the featherless balls of fuzz only a few days old were hostile.

Squalls of pain was heard on all sides, but our Commander signaled for the climb to begin. It was the responsibility of each person to solve his own bird problem. I quickly learned that by unfolding my collapsible entrenching spade, I could brush the birds aside, thus protecting my hands and arms. I also protected my arms by multilayering them with a half dozen pairs of extra socks stored inside my back-pack. My little spade. configured in the shape of a hoe, was a great aid in scaling the steep loose sides of the volcano. My steel helmet protected my head from frequent attacks from birds, when I came too close to their nests upon the ground. I had to use my spade to fend them off.

We began our climb nine o'clock. With that equatorial sun beaming down on us without any source of shade, the stench of guano, the deafening screech of disturbed birds, the constant struggle to make forward progress upon that loose surface, we reached the summit at eleven-thirty, a distance we could have reached in thirty minutes under normal conditions. Salty perspiration, which had drenched our clothing, also caused our numerous oozing wounds to sting.

Due to the geographical isolation from civilization, our fresh water supply to San Cristobal, had to be delivered from a great distance once each month by Navy barge. We were, therefore, limited to one canteen (one quart) of water per day. We could augment that by drinking coffee or tea at the mess-hall, and we could also have a ration of one can of soda or beer per day from the Post Exchange. Ice was unheard of. I carried a couple cans of soft drinks, which I horded and was saving for a time of dire need. At this time, I drank a couple of swallows of water upon reaching the summit, but saved the remainder for additional stress facing us ahead. Our Commander gave us a lunch break, consisting of canned C-rations carried inside our back-packs.

All men present knew that Daphne Major is a volcano, but even our Commander, who assumed the summit would be our turn-around point, was spellbound upon looking inside the crater. At least twice the height of the volcano's outside wall lay the flat sandy crater floor covering perhaps two hundred acres more or less. Peering into the depth of the crater alone gave me a dizzy feeling, but what I also observed really made my head swim. We had already seen thousands of birds during our climb, but that was insignificant compared with what appeared to be a million birds nesting and flying in circles in what a appeared to be perpetual motion. From our eye-level, we estimated the   vertical depth to the floor as being at least of six hundred feet!

Well, no self-respecting Commander was going to pass up that rare once in a life-time opportunity, so we went in. The inside walls had near the same degree of slope as that of the outside. Upon beginning our descent, we encountered the same resistance from the inhabitants, but now, we were buffeted constantly by birds, who were accustomed to colliding with each other. As a result, I had to steady myself with my spade to avoid falling. We had endured a frontal assault upon our upward climb, but now we had to protect our backsides. The deeper we descended into the crater, the more stale became the air and the stench of decaying bodies became unbearable. Without cross-ventilation, the heat of the sun was intense.

We finally reached the floor near two o'clock, observing a landscape alive with bird nests and skeletons, whose depths one can only imagine. One of our officers, being an artilleryman, brought an altimeter for accurately measuring the heights and depths of the island. To our amazement, we were standing a hundred feet below sea level. I spent most of the time holding my nose shut.

Under the circumstances, nobody wished to delay our return to the rim. That required two more hours of most difficult climbing. I was so tired, I truly questioned my ability to make the descent. Half of my water remained, so I finished drinking it before heading for the boats. The last situation we wanted to face would be to still be ashore among those hostile birds after darkness, so we hurried as much as possible. We boarded the boats just as the sun was beginning to set. Our Commander announced that our one assault on Daphne Major would not be repeated.

Who ever started that rumor that Army chow is the most awful food on earth? And was he the same one who circulated the rumor that a steel Army cot with its sagging springs was the worst bed in the world? Just as soon as we returned to Base, I shed those filthy sweaty clothes, skinny-dipped my aching body in the refreshing water of the ocean, and gorged myself on what at the time seemed to be the best food I had ever eaten. A short time later, I died and went to Heaven on my wonderful Army cot.

The Colony

Students of History and Geography know that once explorers discovered that the World is round, creation of a vast sailing ship industry thrived inside Europe, China, and the Middle East. By comparison to modern voyages into outer space, that technology opened the oceans to The Age of Exploration of the here-to-fore unknown world. Greedy Monarchs of nations bordering the Mediterranean and North Seas sent invading armies to conquer and exploit natives whom they considered sub-human in Africa, North and South America, Asia, and all of the island groups of the World. Great Briton, Spain, France, Holland, Portugal, and Germany were the most powerful land-grabbers. They also conducted wars against each other to enforce their territorial claims. Even we Americans, who once were colonized, deposed the Indians and also seized various island groups during an era of territorial expansion. During the Twentieth Century, however, struggles for independence throughout the World resulted a great decline in the number of colonies. Only few continue to exist today. Most of the territories once controlled by the United States were either given independence or became additional States.

The colonial powers usually supervised life inside a colony through the authority of a Governor and an occupying Army. Many governors were cruel tyrants who made life miserable for the natives. The 'mother-country' extracted taxes, forbade commerce with other countries, restricted travel, required the natives to purchase all of their needs from their masters, could not make any laws, could not vote, nor possess the money of another country. At the same time, the natives' countries were made poor by the extraction of their gold, silver, other natural resources , and agricultural production. History in school books provided the occupied territories was slanted toward glorification of the 'mother-country'.

The story I am relating to you at this time has a different concept of colonization, however. The people in this story requested to form a colony. A historian told me that this colony had its beginning during the decade of 1920. From your studies about the country of Norway and from television scenes filmed during the Winter Olympics held there several years ago, you learn that the winters are both extremely cold and beautiful. The nation is ruled by a gentle king , who is greatly loved. There are people, however, who do not wish to be ruled by a king, no matter how kind and lovable he may be. One can only wonder about what urge drives some people to break away and seek a drastic change.

The historian said that twenty eight adults and their families departed Norway much as the Plymouth Rock Pilgrims did. They boarded a ship, which passed through the Panama Canal en route to Guayaquil, Ecuador's largest seaport located on the west coast of South America. Although the volcanic Galapagos Islands owned by Ecuador and located six hundred miles west in the Pacific Ocean were uninhabited except for an exile prison compound ruled by a superintendent, the pilgrims requested and obtained a charter to establish a colony there. The small and only level island was the one where the prison compound no longer existed. It was later occupied during World War II by the US Military as an 'early-warning station'. To deny our World War II enemies knowledge of our exact location, our island had the 'cover' name, Little Seymore. The large volcanic island, which we named Big Seymore, was our nearest neighbor and was also the only one of eleven desert islands, which ever received rainfall, but only upon its southernmost tip. Apparently, some leader of the Norwegian party had explored that remote spot of the Earth and chose it as the site of their colony.

Fortunately for our military base located approximately eighty five miles north of the colony known as Academy Bay, the US Department of the Navy negotiated with the Colony to furnish fresh drinking water to our base, which contained a Battalion of Navy 'Seabees', a flying-boat bomber wing, a run-way to accommodate B-24 Heavy bombers and P-39 fighter planes of the Army Air Corps,

and our US Army Coast Artillery and Antiaircraft Battalion. The
Seabees constructed the necessary water collection and storage facility at the Colony. Once each month, the Navy towed huge barges to
Academy Bay to be refilled. Those already filled would be returned
to supply drinking and cooking water for the base. All shower baths
were supplied with ocean water.

My Artillery Unit was stationed on Little Seymore for nine
months. As we awaited the enemy who never came, most of the
time was spent rather leisurely. A typical day upon that equator location began with five o'clock a.m. revile, thirty minutes to shave and
shower, barracks cleaning and bed-making, breakfast at seven, one
hour physical training, one hour close-order drill and bayonet training, one hour gun drill, and one hour spent cleaning of weapons and
other equipment. Lunch was served at twelve noon. Due to the torrid
heat, all men not needed for critical jobs were given a one hour siesta.
Once each week at beginning at two o'clock, we marched completely
around the island wearing full combat gear. On all other days besides
Sunday, our entire afternoon was spent engaged in sports. Swimming
and fishing in the ocean was popular. Evening chow was at six. Since
there were no towns or civilian population, entertainment was attending movies, listening to radios, reading, and writing letters. We also
practiced beach-landings upon other islands or explored them. With
the days and nights at the equator being exactly the same length, total
absence of rainfall, and bright cloudless skies every day, life became
acutely boring.

I had always been fascinated by airplanes, but had only taken
two flights before coming to the Galapagos. I learned that there were
times when Air Corps pilots who had administrative assignments had
difficulty fulfilling their required monthly hours of flight. They had
to squeeze those hours in the air any way they could. With free 'time
on my hands' one afternoon, I called the Air Corps Base Operations
to inquire if I could get a flight with a pilot whose plane would have
an empty seat. The dispatcher informed me that I could take a flight
if I were present at two o'clock a.m. Of course, I was there ahead
of time.

I had no idea of which type plane I would be riding, but was
delighted to learn that the pilot flew an O-47 photography/reconnais-

sance plane. The mission of such planes was to obtain intelligence information about the enemy by photographing their locations, fortifications, and armament. The two-seated O-47 was equipped with a powerful radial engine and was the fastest photography plane in the Air Corps at that time. The plane looked like a foot-ball shaped greenhouse. Its entire fuselage, excluding its wing and tail areas, flight controls, and camera mounts; consisted entirely of framed glass. The photographer's space which I occupied, faced the tail section. Both the pilot and I had an unobstructed view in every direction including through the floor. I had 'inter-communications' microphone and head-set with the pilot, but could only see him via a mirror mounted above our heads. In the isolated and relatively safe location of Galapagos far from the heavy combat zones of the south-Pacific, the plane was not used very much, thus causing the pilot to strive to fulfill his flight-time requirements.

I could not have been more thrilled. I was taking a flight in one of the Air Corp's most powerful craft capable of fighter plane speed during that era. With no restricted flight plan, as free as a bird, that pilot was in a frisky recreational mood. We could truly climb into 'the wild blue yonder'. Immediately after launching, the pilot asked me if I was comfortable and if I 'wanted to boogie'. I told him that I was comfortable and for him to 'give it his best shot'.

He did. After he cleared any restricted airspace near the established flight paths of the Air Corps and Navy's heavy bombers, he proceeded to practice every flight maneuver he had ever been taught; climbing, diving, rolling, looping. Bound snuggly by my seat-belt, although stressed by several G-forces, all of my body parts remained in their normal positions, except that my stomach was involved in strange gyrations in rhythm with those of the plane, but I was having a ball.

Eventually, the pilot made a level flight circuit of most of the volcanic Galapagos islands, some of which my friends and I had explored earlier by boat. He asked it there was any place in particular I wished to visit. I told him that I would like to fly over Academy Bay Colony. We arrived during the afternoon and circled the area several times at approximately eight hundred feet altitude being careful not to pass directly overhead with such a noisy engine. From my glass house, I could plainly see every detail of the village, as well as the friendly waves by the residents. I felt rewarded to observe an efficient settlement constructed in a 'make-do manner' in such a primitive environment. From the appearance of the buildings, gardens, corral areas, and the farm implements, I was reminded of the life-style of the horse and buggy days of my youth in our farming community among the mountains of West Virginia. I was especially impressed by the salt vats constructed near the ocean's edge, some of which were flooded, while others whose water had evaporated, gleamed with white salt ready for use. I also noted with interest the fresh water impoundment and the Navy barges from which our drinking water at Little Seymore came. Erosion by the small stream, cascading from the towering mountain through a deep ravine over millions of years, eventually created the small harbor where the colonialists anchored their small ocean-going sail boat. After viewing hundreds of miles of arid wasteland and volcanoes, it was refreshing to see even a few thousand acres of green vegetation once more.

I felt a bit forlorn and slightly saddened when we finally left that peaceful village and returned to Base. Sixty two years later at the time of this writing, I cannot help wondering what life is like at that lovely spot. Undisturbed by the modern World's strife, pestilence, and natural disasters, does the World continue to pass those people by unconcerned and unnoticed? Also, there must now be a cemetery containing the remains of some of the earliest citizens near the place where a simple church stood, and there must be babies where only a few existed before. Perhaps there may be some old grand-parents who tell the story of a speeding plane that resembled a flying green-house which spent a few minutes above their village on a balmy afternoon long ago during 1944.

A Promise Kept

The voyage aboard the rusty old steamship from Naples, Italy to Ellis Island, New York during the winter of 1920 was slow, cold, and tiresome for Mamma and Papa Sardello. They were dirt poor, but were dreaming of a life of opportunity in America. First, they would have to defer pursuing the opportunity they dreamed of, because they had signed a contract with the Agent of a wealthy American businessman who owned an ice and coal-yard in New York City. They thus became indentured slaves, each pledging to work ten years for him to pay for their passage to America. Mama agreed to become his house-maid and Papa agreed to work for his business. Their employer provided them a house in which to live plus a small wage for the purchase of food and clothing.

Aboard ship, their meager possessions stored inside a trunk consisted of a few items of clothing and some treasured keep-sakes. One of those treasures was Papa's beloved accordion, which had belonged to his Father, now deceased. Papa was a happy light-hearted man who loved to entertain the other passengers by playing the accordion and singing Italian songs.

Many years later, I met their son, Angelo, at Fort Clayton in Panama, where we were basic trainees in the US Army during World War II. I was saddened to learn that Papa Sardello had died and did not live long enough to realize his American dream. I had not traveled widely at that time, so Angelo told me many stories about his parent's life in Italy and in New York City.

After we completed sixteen weeks of basic training, we were transferred to Fort Amador, a few miles from Fort Clayton to join our first Unit assignment, an anti-aircraft battalion. Following his father's death, Angelo became the proud owner of his father's accordion. After settling into our new Unit, Angelo had his mother ship the acordion to his new address. Papa Sardello had taught his son well, for he played enchanting music with that instrument. Our fellow soldiers and I spent many happy hours listening to him play. It made our arduous duties and loneliness for home much more bearable. In addition to his eternal good nature, that ancient instrument in Antonio's hands seemed to have a soul of its own. My imagination carried me thousands of miles to the great concert halls of Rome, Florence, and Venice, of which I had only heard and would only have opportunity to visit many years later. Angelo's nimble fingers and swaying rhythm conjured images of crowded dance floors of happily waltzing people.

Spending dreary months away from our homes and families gave us the feeling that we were wasting our youth, while our Country was locked into a brutal war, whose end was not in sight. For the moment, the men in our Unit were relatively safe, except for occasional training accidents. There were times when our mission seemed insignificant, but our preparedness was important to the defense of the Panama Canal, should the enemy attempt a sneak attack. To lessen that possibility, the Panama Defense Command created a fan-shaped line of early warning stations hundreds of miles away on both the Atlantic and Pacific sides of the canal. Beginning with Nicaragua north of Panama on the Pacific side, then south to the Galapagos Islands six hundred miles off the coast of Ecuador, thence to Salinas Ecuador, and terminating at Talara Peru.

After a brief stay at Fort Amador, Angelo and I were among those shipped first to Salinas and later to Galapagos during February 1943 aboard a tramp steamer named the USS Johnson. The desert island upon which we were stationed was approximately one mile wide and two miles long, having no natives or towns, and populated by goats, iguanas, huge turtles, and sea-birds. The ocean surrounding it was teeming with every imaginable form of sea-life including sea-lions, manta-rays, electric eels, sharks, and jelly-fish, others to numerous to list. Our food supply was shipped to us monthly aboard the Johnson, and our fresh water was towed in by tanker barge as needed. Other than tea or coffee at the mess-hall, we were rationed one canteen of drinking water daily -- imagine that with the equator only a couple of degrees away. Only sea water ran in our showers, so most men accomplished their sanitary needs by swimming among the sea creatures.

As the Japanese Army and Navy were being pushed away from occupied Pacific territories toward their homeland, the threat to the Panama Canal lessened. One by one the early warning stations were abandoned, Galapagos being among the last. The invasion of Europe now became top priority, so one day without warning and only eight hours advanced notice, three fourths of our Unit received orders to be air-lifted directly to Germany, without any leave-time in the United States. The orders prohibited taking of any personal possessions aboard the planes; only each individual's military clothing and equipment. No time was allowed to mail any possessions home. In fact, due to war-time censorship, revealing troop movements was prohibited. For reasons unknown to me, I was not included in the transfer. By night-fall, our friends were gone and our lonely existence became more lonely.

Poor Angelo was devastated. He was forced to leave his treasured accordion behind. He came to me consumed by grief. What was to become of the accordion? Everyone believed that it would be only a short while until the remainder of our Unit would be evacuated to the States. Angelo and I exchanged home addresses, and he begged me to take his accordion home with me and ship it to him after the war. I promised.

As anticipated, within a month, I returned to the United States with the remnants of our Unit. We were hastily absorbed into another Artillery Battalion at Fort Bragg, North Carolina and shipped to the Philippine Islands to combat the Japanese. We were granted a short leave to visit our homes, during which time, I left Angelo's accordion with my parents with instructions that, if I never returned, ship Angelo's accordion to him after the war.

Six months after the war ended, pleased that I had survived, I was discharged and I returned to my home and Sweetheart at Smoot, West Virginia. Angelo was also on my mind. I immediately used the address he gave me. Rather than take a chance the accordion may be damaged or lost, I wrote a letter to see if Angelo had returned home. Within a week, the letter was returned, Addressee Deceased. A second and a third letter were also returned with the same message. I could only assume that his mother had also died. I hoped that the Postal Department may be mistaken and that some day Angelo would use the address I gave him; that he was alive and well. Sixty one years I have waited to keep my promise, but I am sad to say the letter never came.

I cannot play the accordion, but, if it truly does have a soul, it surely must have pined away every minute of those long years to be grasped once more by Angelo's master hands, yearning to be freed from those confining walls, and to release its loving symphonies again to the listening world. Its current fate is likened to the kinetic potential of the un-hatched egg of a meadow-lark awaiting the release of its rhapsody for all to hear; or the chinned Stradivarius awaiting the lifting of the Maestro's baton. In addition to this, I wish I could hear Angelo's voice say, "Thanks for keeping your promise, Ed."

The Wayward Pig

There is a small village named Alabang located near the foot of a high jungle-covered mountain south-east of Manila on Luzon in the Philippine Islands. It was during July 1945 when a United States 240 mm Field Artillery Battalion of which I was a member arrived there for the purpose of helping to drive the Japanese invaders from the island. A terrible war was happening in the area, during which the islands had been occupied by a Japanese army for three and one half years. Alabang was a pretty little village shaded by coconut palm trees and comprised of quaint bamboo houses built on stilts and sheltered by thatched rice-straw roofs. The natives were farmers whose green rice paddies covered thousands of acres in a lush river valley.

We arrived at Alabang by train from Manila aboard open cattle cars after debarking from a troop ship in Manila Bay. Our Unit established camp upon the only solid ground adjacent to the village and not consisting of rice paddies. We were blessed by a few dry days, during which we moved our heavy vehicles and howitzers into position. After a night of rain, the slightest vehicular traffic turned the area into a quagmire. We lived in tents, but heavy rain soon seeped by osmosis into the floor areas creating more than boot-top deep mud. We also slept upon folding canvas cots whose wooden legs sank into the mud under body weight until the bottom of the canvas rested upon the surface.

When preparing to go to bed, it was futile to pull boots out of the mud when removing them. I would simply maneuver myself to the edge of my cot, unlace my boots, leave them in place, and reinsert my feet into them upon arising the next morning. During any time while wearing boots and standing in the mud, it was necessary several times a day to withdraw a foot from a boot to remove leaches, which had invaded them, and to get relief from their painful bites. That nuisance combined with swarms of mosquitoes was especially annoying, painful, and dangerous when standing perimeter guard. One's life depended upon remaining quiet and unobserved by Japanese infiltrators intent upon killing Americans. They had the advantage of stealth during nights of inky darkness and would take lethal advantage of a sentry exposing himself while pulling off a boot to extract a leach or revealing his position when slapping mosquitoes. The fact was at that stage of the Philippine campaign, the Japanese forces were badly fragmented, starving, and desperately trying to rejoin their own Units from which they had been separated as the result of recent US victories. Reports were that many of them had been successful in killing sentries, raiding US Army kitchen pantries for food, followed by tossing grenades into tents as they were making their escape.

For many of us, that was our first exposure to combat conditions; we simply were unfamiliar with the cunning ways that the enemy used to neutralize us. Soon after our arrival, three of our officers died when a grenade was tossed into their tent while they slept. The first Sunday morning following our arrival, while standing in the out-of-doors breakfast chow-line, one of my friends was felled by a sniper's bullet striking one of his knees. The sniper was hidden by the jungle growth covering the mountain near our camp and was not found or seen.

The residents of Alabang were so accustomed to Japanese raids and brutality, they showed little or no alarm over the incidents involving us. In less than two weeks after our arrival, however, we received news that two hundred rice farmers, including their wives, and children were machine-gunned to death while working in their rice paddies during a day-light raid by Japanese soldiers hiding in that same mountain jungle.

The war with Japan was rapidly coming to an end, and our big guns capable of firing one hundred sixty pound projectiles for twenty two miles, were brought to Luzon to hurry them on their way. It is most unusual for an artillery unit to send out a combat patrol; for that is usually the task of infantrymen or reconnaissance troops. In this instance, however, an order was issued by Corps Headquarters to our Battalion for a specialized artillery forward observation team to move as close as possible to direct accurate fire upon the head-quarters of the fleeing Japanese army located atop that same lengthy mountain located next to our camp. Intelligence reports indicated that a large number of enemy troops had assembled inside deeply bunkered positions from which they were directing attacks upon towns and military positions in the valleys below.

On the morning the order was received, our Commanding Officer informed us that our Battery was chosen to conduct the patrol, which was to span two nights and a day. He told us that he hoped to form the patrol of fifteen men entirely from volunteers in addition to the specially trained forward observer team lead by a Lieutenant. He specified that the men chosen had to be non-smokers, since any odor, especially tobacco smoke, can be smelled for great distances inside a damp jungle. He also stated that in preparation for the patrol, those chosen should bathe thoroughly without applying any type of deodorant, shaving lotion, hair tonic, or insect repellant. No man would chew gum or use toothpaste, or any other perfumed product whose odor could reveal the patrol's location. Each man would carry two canteens of water, which each man would ration to last for the duration of the trip. Only dry K-rations would be carried instead of the C-rations packaged in metal cans that could accidentally rattle. All dog-tags, canteens, extra ammunition clips, and buckles on observation equipment and rifle slings would be taped. Only soft fatigue hats, no helmets would be taken. All exposed skin would be blackened. Since they could reflect sunlight, no person wearing glasses could go on the patrol. Only if under attack would anyone speak aloud while in the target zone. During daylight, communication would be by hand signals only. During darkness, messages would be transmitted by tapping one's nearest comrade on his shoulder and the message whispered and passed on. Total radio silence would be observed, until the pre-designated time for the artillery barrage was scheduled to begin; even then, only subdued volume of voice kept to absolute necessity to complete the mission would be used.

The patrol ate the evening meal and boarded an army truck after the arrival of total darkness. As customary during combat operations, the truck traveled slowly and without lights the several miles to the drop-off location beside a shallow river. That spot's precise location had been previously reconnoitered during daylight in order that the patrol leader would have a specific compass direction to follow upon entering the jungle. By adhering as exactly as possible to the direction and approaching the mountain head-on, we would know when we reached our objective, which simply was the summit. Not an exact science, but being in proximity of our target would be satisfactory, considering that artillery fire can be adjusted both laterally and vertically as necessary. The Lieutenant, by using the illuminated dial of his compass, kept us reasonably on course.

The restrictions involving silence were immediately put into practice, for the only hope of our mission's success was if we reached our target undetected. There was no way of knowing if Japanese troops were also in the vicinity of our planned route. We waded quietly into the river and having crossed it, we moved single-file into the inky-darkness of the jungle. Each soldier stayed within arms-reach of the one in front of him, as the Lieutenant began leading our slow climb.

Traveling without break and under light load, when near midnight, we reached a flat area of approximately ten acres or less only a few hundred feet from the summit. The Lieutenant directed our patrol sergeant to form a circular perimeter defense, thus posting us as guards a few yards apart. We were forbidden to sleep and were instructed to avoid moving about, unless coming under attack.

So far so good. No encounters nor incidents. Everything was just fine until near two o'clock when we were alarmed by a sound one would hear if a metal canteen cap dangled from its chain and struck the side of the canteen. The sound was intermittent and never was distinct. There were times when there was no sound at all followed by several repetitions of it. Needless to say, everyone was nervous and I feared that someone of we non-combat 'green-horn' troops would panic and become 'trigger-happy,' which probably bring a fatal attack upon our small group by the Japanese. The sound seemed to be coming from the area immediately to my front, so I silently inched forward upon my stomach to see if I could determine who or what was making the sound. I did not crawl very far, because I could see nothing over which to be alarmed. We contented ourselves just to await daybreak and see what happened.

When daylight came, all of us were surprised to learn what had made the noise causing such alarm. We were within approximately three hundred feet of a grove of large nut-bearing trees, where a herd of small wild pigs similar to South-American peccaries were feeding. Some Philippine families attach straps and bells upon their pigs and allow them to forage for free food in the jungles and, thus, fattening them for butchering. When it's the right time, they listen for the bell and retrieve their pigs. One, who caused our worry, had joined the herd of wild pigs, but somewhere, the domestic pig had lost the clapper from its bell. As the animals were contentedly harvesting nuts beneath the trees, the empty bell occasionally contacted a tree-trunk or some other object causing the sound we heard.

The discovery of the hog eased our tension, but what else I saw when daylight arrived almost caused me a heart-attack. Within three feet of where I stopped crawling in through the tall grass during darkness was the vertical edge a gapping crevasse at least fifty feet deep, the eroded result of centuries of torrential tropical rains. During our 'sound-out' restrictions, I could have easily disappeared without a sound.

We kept our perimeter defense positions as we quietly ate breakfast and tended our other morning necessities, before resuming the search for our objective. We were pleased to discover that we were well within viewing distance of the Japanese headquarters. We concealed ourselves in the dense foliage until time for the barrage to begin. The fire direction team readied and aimed their equipment without exposing their location. Once more, we remaining soldiers occupied perimeter defense positions. At the precise pre-arranged time, the Lieutenant informed Battalion of our coordinates and called for the first ranging round. Within minutes, a massive explosion appeared beyond the far perimeter of the Japanese location. The Lieutenant quickly called for a reduction in range. The second round fell reasonably short as desired. After a quick calculation, the Lieutenant called for a salvo, which when fired, landed within the desired kill-range. From that moment through the next hour, a heavy barrage plowed the mountain-top as the Lieutenant through his directions swept the barrage backwards, forwards, and side to side until he was satisfied that the entire installation and its personnel were destroyed.

Knowing well that Japanese Infantry units bivouacked outside the target area would began a wide search for our fire-direction patrol, casting most caution to the wind, we made a hasty retreat down the mountainside, hoping to put as much distance between ourselves and our probable pursuers as possible. Since there were no existing trails through that area of the mountain, we had little fear that the Japanese could travel any faster than ourselves and they could only guess the direction of our travel, We did not want to be fool-hardy, but the farther we put our original position behind us, the safer we felt.

It was early evening when we reached the river. We did not wish to expose our truck and driver to a possible Japanese ambush when he arrived, so once more we concealed ourselves in a defensive position inside the edge of the jungle and waited for darkness. The Lieutenant requested the driver not be dispatched to arrive until nine o'clock. Near seven-thirty, the Lieutenant sent a few soldiers at a time across the river to take rear-defensive positions several yards apart along the opposite side of the road in order to defend others until all were safely across.

Japanese soldiers did not arrive. Our driver along with several more armed men came at nine o'clock and we returned to our Unit without anyone receiving even a blister or a scratch. As for myself, I was pleased for the experience and was a bit proud of myself for having actually made a patrol as an artilleryman. I have often thought about that night and the pig. I have also thought about the little village of Alabang and wondered what it must be like now sixty-one years later and if those houses resembling wicker baskets still stand there.

So You Want to Become a Paratrooper

It is not easy to make the decision to become a paratrooper. You just do not awaken some morning and say I think I will jump out of an airplane today. As for myself, if the opportunity ever occurred, I wanted to become a paratrooper. The opportunity materialized during 1950 when the Korean War began and I was recalled to the Army. I was not pleased to be recalled nor did I wish to be separated from my family facing the prospect of returning to combat. After having served almost four years during World War II, I was in college, was twenty nine years old, had been married four years, and had a two year old son. Although I had never been 'airborne', I became assigned to Battery B, 675th Airborne Field Artillery Battalion, Fort Campbell, Kentucky for 'refresher training'. There was nothing that I could do about returning to the Army, but, if I had to be there, how lucky could I get? Here was my chance to become a paratrooper.

Aside from wanting to be a paratrooper, one had to be in excellent physical condition and he must volunteer. No one forces a person to 'go airborne', but should he ever refuse to jump, he could not spend another night with his unit. He would be transferred before the end of the day. There can be no 'quitters' in an airborne Unit. On January 2, 1951, I, along with a large group of other volunteers, was shipped by train to the famous Airborne Jump School at Fort Benning, Georgia. Upon arrival, I was appointed as a platoon leader.

Jump School at that time lasted three weeks. The first week was spent in airborne indoctrination and building of physical endurance. Each day began at five o'clock with a two mile in-step run in company formation before breakfast. Meals were served at seven AM, noon, and six PM. Each member of a Company's Training Cadre carried a clip-board at all times containing the name of each trainee. Alongside each name was an assigned number, which also was also stenciled in three inch high digits upon the front of the individual's steel airborne helmet. That number tracked each trainee's success or failure throughout the three week period. All troop movements as well as individual movements were at a run. If caught walking or even making the slightest mistake, the individual was fined either twenty push-ups or set-ups to be performed on the spot.

When not busy in physical training, we were kept busy making parachute landing falls from six foot high wooden platforms by jumping forward, backward, or to both sides. We also practiced mock parachute guiding maneuvers alongside dozens of other men while suspended for an hour in parachute harness dangling from the rafters of open-sided buildings. Thereby, we practiced slipping the parachute to either side, front, and back avoiding hazards and targeting the spot where the jumper hoped to land. When not engaged in performing the above, we were strapped into a real parachute, required to lie upon our backs, and scooted across the ground at approximately fifteen miles per hour by the inflated parachute filled by wind produced by a stationary engine powered propeller. This simulated frequently encountered actual windy conditions when making a landing. It was called 'recovery from the drag', accomplished by forcefully pulling on either one of two harness risers into one's abdomen area and at the same time bringing both knees into contact with one's chest. Doing that resulted in reversing one's direction of travel, causing him to spin upon his shoulder-blades and being hoisted his feet by the wind into a running position. Having accomplished this, the jumper circles ahead of his open parachute, thus spilling its air and causing it to collapse upon the ground. A final activity of first week training is performed by loading the trainees inside a mock airplane fuselage to perform the in-flight safety checks and exiting techniques, culminating in the commands of "stand up, hook-up, make an equipment safety check of the man behind and in front of you, shuffle, and stand in the door." Each man is given an individual 'tap-out' using a pre-instructed exit routine, that is, pretending to be leaping from a plane, bring his feet together, head down, and elbows tight against the jumper's sides, shouting a four-second count of "one thousand, two thousand, three thousand, four thousand", followed by looking upward to determine if the imaginary parachute is fully open or dangerously damaged. In the case of a seriously torn or tangled parachute, the jumper is trained to turn his head to his left and pull the ripcord of the reserve parachute attached to his chest harness.

Second week was consumed by all of the physical training routines of the previous week, but now our courage and determination was seriously tested by repeated daily jumps from thirty four foot high 'mock-up jump simulator towers' equipped with airplane doorways. The only equipment we wore were our steel airborne helmets, pistol belts, and canteens for water. Every man had to complete at least five daily 'graded' qualifying jumps from the towers, if he hoped to move on to week three.

Before standing in the door, each trainee is strapped into a parachute harness, which is attached to a little trolley device attached permanently to a steel cable an inch in diameter extending approximately one hundred yards, where it is anchored to a stout wooden post positioned atop a ten foot high earthen mound. It is similar to what is commonly referred to as a 'death slide'. If it were not for all of the running, climbing, instructors shouting, and constant 'push-ups', jumping from the thirty four foot towers would be fun. I really enjoyed the trolley rides.

We were required to stand in the door and assume the proper exit position with one foot slightly behind the other, knees slightly bent, hands holding the sides of the door, head and eyes straight forward. We were required to shout our last name and our three digit identification number to a sergeant standing upon the ground below holding a clip-board containing our Company's roster. When he acknowledged the jumper's identity, the 'jump-master' standing alongside the trainee would slap him forcefully on his back-side and shout "go!" That is the point where most 'quitters' refuse to exit. One student in my platoon balked each time he stood in the door. To acquaint him with the experience of having exited the door, the jump-master pushed him out the door a few times when he returned from the trolley ride, but he never overcame his fear. He would hump in the doorway and say, "Hit me one more time Sarge, I'm gonna go this

time", but he finally sat on the floor and was given a failing grade.

When a jumper made a forceful exit from the door, he would pull hard upon the sides of the door, attempt to jump upward, grasp the ends of his reserve parachute while forcing his elbows to his sides, scissors his feet together , hold his chin tightly against his chest, and shout loudly "one thousand, two thousand, three thousand, four thousand", the four seconds required for a parachute to normally open. All of that having been done, the jumper spreads the parachute harness risers wide apart, while looking upward as he would when actually jumping to determine if the parachute is damaged. Also pretending if it is damaged, he turned his head to the left and pretended to pull the rip-cord of his reserve parachute mounted upon his chest. By that time, the jumper is approaching the earthen mound at high speed. To earn a passing grade, he must accomplish all of the above procedures prior to crossing a lime stripe across the glide path on the ground. Failure to meet all of those requirements results in repeated attempts, until the student makes five perfect jumps. Other men are standing atop the mound to grab the speeding jumper to prevent him from crashing into the anchor pole. As soon as the student could extract himself from the harness, he had to run to the grading sergeant to learn if he had either made a satisfactory jump or failed.

The final day of week two was spent being strapped into a real parachute at the base of one of four two hundred fifty foot tall steel towers with cross-arms capable of dropping four jumpers simultaneously. That procedure began by donning the harness while the parachute lay deflated upon the ground. When ready, a steel cable is dropped from one of the arms for each trainee and his parachute is hoisted by its apex to the top of the tower by an electric motor. A grading sergeant on the ground beneath each arm controls the automatic release for his individual student and evaluates his performance as he drifts downward. Using a 'bull-horn' the sergeant communicates commands to slip forward, backward, right, and left. He then observes the jumper to determine the correctness of his parachute landing fall (PLF). At that point in a 'trooper's training, few have any problems with this enjoyable experience, which can also be had at New York's Coney Island Amusement Park.

Week three arrived before daylight on Monday morning after a week-end of soul-searching and reality checks. By Sunday evening, we trainees assigned to my platoon sat quietly staring into the distance. With little conversation, most seemed like convicts facing execution at day-break. Realizing that each of us had to make five qualifying jumps from a plane in order to earn our 'wings', failure would mean that all of the hard work would have been in vain. The rule was, if a student actually performed any or all of the jumps, but failed to make a passing grade, he could, if he chose, repeat the entire course. If, however, he refused to jump, that was unforgivable.

That cold January morning arrived with a four o'clock 'rise and shine'. My breakfast felt like a brick in my stomach. I deliberately ate little, fearing that the tension may cause me to become sick. We boarded canvas-covered trucks for the ride to Lawson Air-field located a few miles distance. Each of us wore our steel jump helmets and eighty five pounds of combat equipment. Upon arrival, we entered a huge warehouse called the 'sweat-shed', where tens of thousands of parachutes were packed and stored inside large bins. As we passed the issuing officer's table, each was given a back-pack main parachute and a reserve parachute. We formed a line of two rows twenty one men each. We paired into two man teams and assisted each other getting dressed. The main parachute weighs approximately twenty pounds and the reserve weighs approximately ten pounds.

Each partner helps his buddy into the harness by threading the leg straps through those of one's combat pack, which no longer is worn upon his back, but now hangs in front over the trooper's thighs. The parachute's shoulder and leg straps are then snapped into a quick-release position at the middle of the jumper's chest. Once the harness is tightened so much that the jumper has difficulty breathing and standing erect, the safety belt is threaded through loops on the back side of the reserve parachute after it has been snapped to the main one. The reason the harness is so tightly drawn is that the opening shock outside the plane is so violent, should the harness be slack, it will peel strips of skin off one's body.

Once the equipment had been donned and inspected by the Jump-master, we marched single file and boarded our plane. The engines were idling, but the wind from the ten foot long propellers caused me to stagger as we walked behind them. There were canvas jump-seats mounted upon pipe frames which extended the full length on each side of the cargo space from the jump doors to the wall of the pilot's compartment. Two half inch diameter steel cables extending the full length the cargo compartment were mounted two feet in front of and seven feet above each row of seats. Twenty one jumpers faced twenty one others crowded upon those uncomfortable seats. The pilot wasted no time taxing to the take-off point. Even on the ground, the engine noise through those un-insulated walls was deafening. One of my men, who had never ridden a plane before, asked me "How high are we now?" when the pilot revved the engines to full throttle at the launch point prior to take-off. I didn't have time to answer, when the pilot released the brakes and the plane raced down the run-way. I placed fingers into each of my ears to shut out the noise. The landing gear nested into its in-flight position with a thud as the plane leveled at our designated fifteen hundred foot jump altitude, was throttled back to cruising speed, and the noise level decreased to almost normal conversation level.

We flew for approximately thirty minutes, when a red light came on above the jump door and the Jumpmaster shouted "Stand Up". At that time I saw through a port hole that two other planes also were flying so close alongside ours that their wing tips appeared to almost touch. We stood as erect as possible and faced the rear of the plane. He shouted, "Hook up", upon which we snapped the hooks at the end of our static lines onto the overhead steel cables, and inserted the safety pins designed to protect them from accidentally un-snapping. The fifteen foot long static lines are S-folded and held in place on the back of our parachutes by rubber bands in such a manner that once the jumper exits the plane, his weight unwinds line to its extremity, thus, automatically pulling the parachute by its apex from the back-pack allowing it to fill with air.

The Jumpmaster shouted, "Check equipment!" Buddies once more made certain there was no safety threat to each other's equipment. The Jumpmaster followed that with the command, "Sound off equipment check", whereupon each trooper shouted "Number one OK, number two OK, in progression until every man was accounted for. That was immediately followed by the command, "Shuffle and stand in the door."

The first exit in Jump School is unlike any other, in that each man stops in the door for two seconds and the Jumpmaster gives him an individual tap-out and shouts "Go", just as was done at the thirty four foot towers the previous week. In order to avoid aborting the flight or endangering the other jumpers, anyone who refuses to jump is pushed aside into the plane's tail cone allowing the next man in line to stand in the door.

There were dozens of jump-school graders positioned on the ground throughout the drop zone with clipboards in hand awaiting the student jumpers arrival. As a general rule, if a man had shown enough courage to jump and was able to walk after landing, he was given a passing grade. Only those who did something totally outlandish endangering themselves were awarded a question mark deserving close observation during later jumps that week. I, along with hundreds of others, made a satisfactory first jump. There was no more glumness at the barracks that night. Everyone was talking at once. After my euphoria wore off, however, it was reality check time again. I had jumped and realized how great was the danger, I truly wondered if I had enough courage to make the second jump the following day. I shall always remember the needless dread of that second jump. It took all of my determination to exit that door, but I made it along with the three other qualifying jumps. Now I knew that I could do it the dread was gone and anticipation abounded.

My fifth jump was almost a disaster, however. On that flight, I was the last man in line on my side of the plane. Some of the jumpers ahead of me took more time exiting than necessary, thus causing me to be late. Traveling at one hundred fifty knots per hour, the plane travels a long way in forty two seconds. My parachute opened and I was thrilled that this was going to be the jump which would earn me my silver wings. But when I looked down, I was horrified to discover that I was far off the drop zone above the dense forest along the Chattahoochee River! I quickly realized that I had no time to waste, so I climbed my risers like a monkey, thus slipping my parachute toward the drop zone. I climbed so far that my hands were almost grasping the nylon edge of the canopy. It was fortunate for me that a slight breeze was blowing in the direction I was slipping. I was falling so fast that I had to lift my legs to avoid tripping upon the final treetops at the edge of the drop zone. Having to make such a hard slip. My parachute was gliding like a plane preparing to crash, when all of my weight was borne by my left leg as I struck the ground with a force which made my ears ring. Without any possibility of making the appropriate landing routine, I cart-wheeled across the ground rolling into and being bound by my parachute. I had a terrible pain in my left hip. I lay upon my back momentarily to assess my bodily damage. I had assumed that I was being watched as I tried to discover if I had any broken bones, when I heard a gruff voice demand, "Are you going to lie there all day soldier?" I struggled to my feet while trying release myself from the parachute.

"No sergeant," I replied as I gingerly pretended that I was not hurting and began stuffing my parachute into my kit-bag. I was certain that the sergeant had been tracking my progress after I left the plane. I think that he knew and I knew that I had performed a miracle.

"Well, gather your gear and double time off the field", he said.

I complied while dreading to hear that had I failed and would have to repeat the entire three weeks work. As I departed upon the two mile jog to the parachute turn-in point with a sad heart, it helped to relieve it and my aching hip when the sergeant shouted, "By the way Martin, you passed."

A World of White

At that stage of my military career during December 1952, I was a Battery Clerk assigned to Battery B, 675th Airborne Field Artillery Battalion. My duty was to prepare the Unit's daily statistical report, type the First Sergeant's duty assignments, maintain files and regulations, and write correspondence for the Battery Commander.

It was that December when our Unit was among the fifteen thousand man 11th Airborne Division moving from Fort Campbell, Kentucky to Camp Drum, New York for a winter maneuver to test the latest Artic cold-weather clothing and equipment. The plan was to make a massive parachute assault during mid-January at Camp Drum and spend the remainder of the winter maneuvering against another Division along the US side of the St. Lawrence River. Upon the Division's arrival, however, snow on the ground was fifty two inches deep. It appeared that the deep snowfall would delay the parachute jump.

Every thing was in a state of delayed readiness, when Nature gave us a surprise. The Thursday night before our scheduled jump date, the sky became cloudless and the temperature suddenly warmed above freezing, reducing the snow to approximately one foot of slush. Nature, however, was not ready to play nice. By Saturday afternoon, a new cold front moved in, dropping the temperature below zero degrees Fahrenheit. The foot of slush, having been churned by traffic inside Camp Drum, became distorted solid ice, making both foot and vehicular travel almost impossible.

The gung-ho never say die Commanding General of the 11th Airborne Division was not about to let weather defeat his plans. We had traveled there for winter maneuvers, and that was winter in its purest form. We were scheduled to begin jumping at six o'clock on the next Monday morning. A Saturday visit by maneuver officials to the drop-zone where nothing man-made had disturbed the former slush, however, revealed thousands of acres resembling a huge plate-glass mirror. Nature was not through taunting us, for on Saturday night, an inch of dry powder snow fell upon the ice.

Normally, jumpers carried their parachutes and combat equipment to the plane upon which they were scheduled to ride. They would stand beneath the wing and don their gear, but the Commanding General feared that a deep body chill and cold stiff hands would render the jumpers incapable of guiding the open parachutes or being able to pull their reserve parachute's rip-cord if the main one malfunctioned. He therefore directed that on Sunday every jumper in the Division would be marched to huge unused airplane hangers with their parachutes and gear. Each company, battery, or troop aligned themselves in the order in which they would board their planes and stepped off an open space between each rank. Each man put on his parachute, adjusted it to fit, and lay it and his combat gear bearing his name upon the floor at his feet. That arrangement enabled each man to put his equipment on, have it given the normal safety checks inside the warm hangers, and to simply walk to his Unit's assigned plane the following morning.

There was nothing common-place about the cold-weather clothing we were going to test. Almost every item was double that which we normally wore. We were issued a fluffy wool liner capable of covering our ears to be inserted to our jump-helmets, our usual field-jacket now had a cozy pile liner with thousands of minute air pockets and a wolf-fur collar, and beneath our field trousers, we wore the same pile-lined insert trousers held up by suspenders. Worn next to skin was thermo underwear beneath a wool shirt. Wearing all of that fluffy garb caused me to think I looked like the Pillsbury Doughboy. We were told to also wear our leather dress gloves, in addition to a massive pair of artic mittens with partial arm sleeves. Each mitten had a long nylon strap sewn to it. To prevent losing the mittens (which we were informed cost the Government $35 per pair fifty four years ago at the date of this writing) from becoming lost, the straps, equipped with connecting fasteners, were threaded through the shoulder epaulets of our field jackets. Frozen hands would occur if the mittens were lost.

One thing that none of us had ever done was jump without our prized paratrooper boots. Of course, they would be inadequate to prevent our feet from freezing during exposure to such frigid weather. In their place, we were issued a pair loose-fitting insulated rubber artic mukluks capable of holding two one-half thick felt insoles and two pairs of heavy woolen socks. They were warm and comfortable for ordinary winter wear, but they were not designed nor suitable for parachute jumping, even with a man not carrying a heavy load. The trouble was, none of us were jumping without a heavy load. They became the immediate worry of each jumper.

The weather remained unchanged. The glistening snow and ice was almost blinding in the bright sunlight of Monday morning. The wisdom of the General's decision to dress ourselves inside the hanger was truly profound, since the temperature when the first troops began jumping at six o'clock was twenty two degrees below zero. Two orders of caution were issued before the jump began. For fear that men could not grip the parachute risers nor feel the emergency parachute rip cord while wearing the bulky mittens, only the uniform leather dress gloves were to be worn until the jumpers reached the ground. The straps attached to the mittens allowed them to flap harmlessly in the air without losing them. Equally important, each man was warned not to stand before releasing his parachute harness from his body. Ignoring that warning while standing upon ice may result in serious injury, should a breeze re-inflate the parachute.

Many planes, including the one upon which I rode, departed the air-field before daylight. As was customary during mass jumps, three planes flew in a V-formation along with two other V-formations, thus forming one wave of twelve planes in a V-of-Vs. Each plane carried forty two jumpers, thus delivering five hundred forty jumpers per wave. Each plane flew at an altitude of fifteen hundred feet at one hundred fifty six knots per hour.

I have no idea of which wave our plane was in, but I know that it was not near the lead wave. We had performed all of the in-flight safety inspections, had arisen from our seats, and hooked our static-lines to the over-head anchor cable. The red light signaling that we were approaching the drop-zone was burning. The mump-master had taken his position in the open doorway awaiting the lighting of the green light signal to begin jumping. I was standing next behind the jump-master on our side of the plane, when the pilot announced over the inter-com that there were so many injuries on the drop-zone, our wave would have to circle around for an additional thirty minutes before jumping. From my position, I had a wide view of the drop-zone where I could see dozens of litter-helicopters landing to evacuate injured troopers. The pilot made an additional announcement instructing the jump-master not to permit the jumpers to return to their seats, for fear that someone may accidentally pop the rip-cord of his reserve parachute, which might snake out an open door, and cause the plane to crash The two exit doors remained open during the entire turn-around flight. The jump-master permitted us to back-step to our original positions inside the plane and to slip our hands into the artic mittens until the red light would be relit. The cold air entering the open doors was numbing.

Our time to exit came and I could still see helicopters searching the drop-zone for injured men. The green light came on and we began our exit. Except for the extreme cold, the process of that jump was no different than many others I had made. My exit was normal and my parachute opened perfectly. One departure from the norm was that, due to the reduced buoyancy of the cold air, everyone fell like rocks.

My problem as to how I would avoid destroying my feet when those rubber shoes touched the ice consumed my thoughts. There was no problem with wind and I had plenty of room among the other falling troopers, so I formulated a plan to look down at my feet, allow my legs to go as limp as possible, while holding them together. My hands were adequately warm, so with a high firm grip upon the risers, I did a strong pull-up and forced my hands into my mid-rift the instant my feet touched the surface in an effort to partially reverse my fall. It worked, but instead of making my normal parachute-landing-fall and tumble, I saw both of my feet fly past my face as though they were going into outer space. In a fraction of a second, I sat down with a violent thump. I didn't have long to decide if I had broken my back. I was still locked into my parachute harness and a near-by litter-helicopter approximately ten feet above the ground was coming toward me. I postponed my physical examination, quickly lay flat, and activated the quick-release of my parachute harness.

Examination of my physical condition was further delayed when I saw one of my friends near-by appearing to be in shock and standing erect with his parachute harness still attached. I was waving frantically for the helicopter pilot to move away, but he apparently did not see me. At the same time, I was yelling to my friend to lie upon the ground. Events were happening too fast. Before I had time to tackle my friend, the chopper re-inflated his parachute, viciously yanking him off his feet, and breaking an arm. A white shaft of bone projected from the wrist band of his jacket. I helped load his gear upon the helicopter while the medics strapped him to the litter cot attached the helicopter's landing skid. I then had time to take inventory of myself. I felt bruised and shaken, but was otherwise intact.

I gathered my belongings and delicately walked upon the ice the two miles to our designated assembly area. All the time, the air was filled with wave after wave of additional jumpers. Along the way, I saw an unconscious soldier hanging in a dead tree as rescuers were freeing him. His picture filled the front cover of Life Magazine the following week.

My Unit boarded awaiting trucks, where the only shelter provided us was the canvas covering the cargo beds. The time was approximately nine o'clock. The convoy lumbered along at approximately fifteen miles per hour until two o'clock the following morning. Our Unit's trucks entered a large field across the highway from the darkened residence of a large dairy farm. Large icicles hanging from the eves of the house gleamed like jewels in the light of a full moon. We moved our stiff bodies off the trucks and immediately began erecting a warming tent. Within minutes, orders came via radio to position our 105mm howitzers into firing order and, using gun powder only, to begin firing an artillery preparation against an imaginary enemy located ten miles away.

Can you imagine being sound asleep in your home at three o'clock and be awakened by artillery fire almost inside your front lawn? When the order to fire was given, I was looking at that house. Lights came on and window sashes flew open in three rooms facing us as heads and shoulders appeared. One of our officers approached the house and apologized to the startled family.

We remained in that farmer's field for two days. Surprisingly, the family was friendly with us and more than a little curious about us and our equipment. They worried about us sleeping outside in the cold. We assured them that we were prepared to survive the weather. The farmer offered to let anyone who wished to sleep inside his barns, but we declined for fear someone would start a fire and destroy the buildings. The farmer insisted that we allow him to donate bales of straw to place beneath our double-insulated down-filled sleeping bags. That we accepted. The farmer told us the roads had been impassable for several days and that his milk tanks were full. It had been impossible to transport his milk supply to market, so of necessity, the milk was being poured upon the ground. He offered and we gladly accepted all the milk we wanted.

The maneuver lasted until mid-March. Except for the necessity of a headquarters tent, a kitchen tent, and occasional warming tent, most men created their own shelters by using lean-to wind-breaks made of pine-tree boughs, digging holes into the banks of snow drifts, or by building igloos. Building and living inside igloos was fun. Usually four men would occupy an igloo. If time and snow depth permitted, they would select a level spot during late afternoon. Using their entrenching-tools, they would cut cinder-block sized blocks of snow from the ground forming a circular area approximately twelve feet or more in diameter. The blocks would be set end to end around the edge of the circle. Outside the circle, additional blocks were cut and stacked upon the first until forming a circular wall approximately four feet high. Tree boughs were cut to form a domed roof, which was packed on top with approximately eight inches of snow. A fire would be built far enough away from the structure to avoid causing it to melt. Trash cans or an open-topped barrel placed over the fire was used to collect and melt snow. Waiting until near darkness to encourage freezing, the cooled water created by melted snow was poured over the entire igloo to seal cracks and to strengthen the structure by freezing. On the down wind side of the igloo, a small opening would be cut into its base as a crawl-through doorway. A short tunnel the height of the entryway would be built through which to crawl, thus avoiding the entry from being blocked by a heavy snow fall or by drift.

It was always advisable for the sake of comfort and safety from frostbite to install a ground-cover when sleeping out of doors during cold weather. Pine boughs make a good barrier between the frozen ground and one's sleeping gear. A piece of tarpaulin or the soldier's shelter-half pup-tent should be placed atop the pine boughs as a water-proof barrier, followed by the soldier's inflated air-bag, and lastly, a double walled artic sleeping bag and blanket.

One of the most important defenses against frost-bite immediately upon rising in the morning, is to inspect the exterior of the waterproof sleeping-bag cover and also the shelter half for patches of frost. The frost must not be melted by any means, but rather, a knife blade should be used to scrape away the frost. If the frost is allowed to remain, or if it is allowed to melt in place, that wet spot will act as a cold conduit the following night, which under extreme conditions might cause frost-bite. The least harm caused will be partially reduced cold resistant capability of the sleeping bag.

To bring this story to a close, we were not under a structural roof for most of three months with most temperatures below zero and in some waist-deep snows. My statistical 'morning-reports' done by typewriter with four carbon copies were a problem at first. Attempting to write them in a cold headquarters tent with cold hands was a challenge. Also, I discovered that carbon paper is critically cold natured. Each time I removed a sheet of carbon paper from its shipping carton, it rolled up like a window-blind and could not be flattened. I faced a dilemma, because there was a dead-line for the report to reach Battalion Headquarters each morning and tardiness was not tolerated. I reasoned that, if the carbon paper liked heat, then I must find a way to provide it. I simply started the engine of our Headquarters truck, turned on its heater, and placed my typewriter on a draw-board recessed beneath the dash-board on the truck's passenger side, and typed away. The carbon paper lay flat and behaved itself.

I also learned that, if I did not want my tooth paste to turn to ice, my shaving cream to refuse to come out of its tube when needed, or my canteen of water to burst, I had better take each of them into my sleeping bag at night. Also, a warming tent was a good place to shave in comparison to attempting to do it outside. Allowing beards to grow was not allowed.

I didn't see any Army Recruiters in action during that maneuver. Perhaps they were a part the home-guard remaining at good ole warm Fort Campbell. Other than missing my wife and children, after awhile, I hardly minded the cold weather at all.

Avalanche

Oberammergau is a quaint sleepy picture-postcard village located among the Alps Mountains in Bavaria, one of the southern states of Germany. I had the privilege of visiting the village numerous times, when I was stationed with the United States Army at Augsburg. I was also fortunate to be a student at the Army's foreign language school located there on two occasions, each lasting three months.

The crooked narrow cobble-stone streets of Oberammergau weave serpent-like between buildings, many of whose exterior walls are covered by colorful murals and whose roofs are made of red masonry tiles. The village, outlined against the backdrop of verdant green pines, linden trees, pool-table green hillside pastures, and granite snow-covered spires of the Alps, is a place of natural beauty.

As is customary in Germany, many of the homes and business places along the streets are combined with barns for the family milk-cows. It was a common sight to see cows followed by milkmaids exiting doors opening onto streets and merging into traffic following morning milking time. It was the chore of milk-maids to herd the cows to the family pastures adjacent to the village. Soon the cows, wearing their merrily ringing bells, could be seen grazing peacefully upon the green sides of the foot-hills. During the late afternoons, the returning cows would appear to be window-shopping as the milk-maids drove them, bodies wagging and tails swishing, until each one arrived at its familiar door, awaiting it to be opened for another comfortable night. During the extremely heavy snow falls of winter, the pasturelands were deserted and the cows remained inside. Just as was customary during the early days in America, the dung-heaps were piled outside behind the barn until used for fertilizer on summer crops.

It was during the winter of 1965 that this story had its beginning. I had already attended school for two months, eight hours per day. Winter days in Bavaria are gloomy and foggy most of the time, becoming so dark on days of heavy snowfall that street lights are often turned on. Our classes began at seven o'clock and we were dismissed at four. I was a paratrooper accustomed to vigorous activity every day back at my home base. Being cooped inside a building all day nearly drove me insane. Do understand that most of the 'ground-pounding' soldiers who were my classmates were happy to exert themselves as little as possible. Being a West Virginian, I could not tolerate seeing a mountain standing unclimbed. Every evening, come rain, shine, or snow, I was out of doors as long as daylight lasted and many times after dark. I also loved the atmosphere of German restaurants (called Gasthouses) and I enjoyed practicing my newly learned language in conversations with the natives so as to tune my ears to the way it was supposed to be spoken. I usually walked down the mountain into town after dinner each evening for a couple of hours, before retiring to my room to study until two o'clock in the morning.

A paved two-lane highway leading to the vacation world of Garmish passed through Obberammergau and crossed a high mountain named Etal. Two miles up the mountain from the village was the remote Etal Monastery, their Closter, gasthaus, and their Etaler Brewery. Yes, brewery, because many monasteries in Europe earn their existence by making beer or wine. Etal was the first monastery I had visited and I was fascinated by that way of life so unfamiliar to me. I absorbed the silence of those massive ancient moss-covered walls and the long verandas facing the court-yard flower garden maintained with the neatness of a book-keeper's ledger. The aroma of the gasthaus, the ghostly shadows cast by flickering candles dancing across massive wooden tables and brown-clad monks speaking with almost inaudible tones among themselves and their guests; the chime of a silver bell calling the monks to worship; the many voices sounding as only one as the monks sang their devotion in Gregorian Chant mesmerized me as though I was in another world. I often hiked those two miles to Etal to eat a snack and to absorb the mysteries of that beautiful peaceful place.

One winter day, the outside air suddenly warmed and the snow, which had lain for weeks, compacted to no more than a foot in the valley, but could have been fifty or more feet on the mountain tops and glaciers. The bright sunshine drew me like a magnet. During break periods all afternoon, I tried to coax some of the other men to join me in a hike after school, but my urging fell upon deaf ears. I learned to be self-reliant early in life, so, as was my practice, I stashed my books in my room, dressed in hiking gear, and journeyed through the pastureland above the school in the direction of a granite peak atop Etal Mountain. I did not wait for dinner, since I wanted to cover as much distance as possible before dark. I satisfied my thirst by eating snow and carried only some dehydrated fruit and nuts. I planed to turn east across a deep ravine and hike through the dense evergreen forest to the Etal Monastery, where I planned to eat dinner before returning to base.

I was scarcely out of sight of the military compound, when I startled a herd of approximately thirty Hirsch deer. They are short-legged stocky built animals with rather large horns much like a Rocky Mountain sheep of North America. I assume they received their name because of the loud hissing sound made when they are alarmed. It sounds like a prolonged Hirsch-ch-ch. I was pleased that I flushed the herd, because climbing through the snow that first compacted under my weight and then collapsed with each step was very tiring. The herd proceeded me up the mountain in single file, thus making their path almost bare to the ground. Every couple of hundred yards, they would stop and look to see if I was continuing to follow. I also took comfort in the fact that where ever they could climb, I, too, could follow without any special equipment.

Satisfaction with my good luck further increased, when the deer took a right turn across the ravine, which I had plan to cross. Without their help, I probably would have turned back after observing how difficult my progress would have been in through it in the dimming light of approaching darkness. I carried a strong flashlight inside my parka, but I had hoped to reach the monastery before the time of deep darkness through the pine forest. I was so grateful for the help the sheep had been to me, so I didn't really mind hiking the mile remaining before reaching my destination.

Then, it happened. I had barely cleared the ravine a few feet, when the deers' movement triggered a small avalanche! It began with the cracking of broken limbs and quickly grew into a deafening roar as it whizzed past me at what must have been fifty miles per hour, but confining itself to the ravine. In my trembling amazement, my eyes bulged at the sight of rocks and trees crashing with the sound of rifle shots, then came silence. Total silence. Total, that is, except for the thumping of my heart. It was racing so fast my pulse was thumping in my ears.

I realized that I had narrowly escaped disappearing forever and nobody would have ever known what happened to me. After walking to the monastery, I sat in deep thought, while I slowly ate dinner. Sitting there in the warmth of that wonderful place, I realized that I had 'dodged a bullet' one more time. I had seen danger in many forms during my past, but I knew that I still loved mountains and that I would continue to climb them every chance I could. I simply promised myself that I would not tempt fate in exactly that same manner again.

My Day On Der Korper

I had spent eight hours per day in a classroom for three long months studying the German Language at the US Army's Language School at Oberammergau in Bavaria. Each day, I could see the lofty snow-capped peaks of the Alps Mountains appearing to touch the sky beyond the valley and the red topped buildings of that quaint little village. Much closer and just outside the village limits, was the towering solitary peak of solid rock the Germans named Der Korper (the statue). It rose straight out of the valley floor to an altitude of approximately two thousand feet, its base separated from the lawns of the village by the narrow head-waters of the Ammer River. Der korper was round and came to a point resembling the upside-down shape of a huge icicle or a giant totem pole made of granite.

From where I sat in class each day, I could see what appeared to be a small cross projecting from the tip of Der Korper. During the heavy snows of winter, the peak really did resemble a huge icicle. Great drifts would gather atop the hundreds of stone ledges and crags lining all of its sides. When the ledges became so filled with snow they could hold no more, the howling winds would dislodge the drifts sending mini-avalanches free falling through the blustery air blotting Der Korper completely from view. With the coming of spring, the snow quickly melted into the small river below. The bright rays of the sun revealed the gleaming gray/white granite contrasting beautifully with the dark green foliage of the trees. Appealing to the West Virginia mountaineer heart within me, Der Korper seemed to beckon by some silent telepathy, "Come to me. Come to me."

I waited impatiently for the weather change to come, which would allow me to safely climb Der Korper. Its sides are so steep, I wondered if I really could climb it without special climbing gear I did not have. A German mountaineer said to me, "Ach, Der Korper is just a baby mountain." One of the language professors told me that he had organized groups of students throughout previous years, who climbed the peak with him, but none of in my classmates had any interest in doing it. The date of my graduation was rapidly approaching, so if I were going to climb that beautiful peak, I would have do it alone.

The spring weather was becoming warm and beautiful. One Saturday night, I began making preparation to begin my climb early the next morning. I packed the clothing and light gear I would need, including food and water. I planned to leave campus long before breakfast so to arrive at the base of the mountain before daylight. The next morning, I signed myself out at the school office before four o'clock. I had told my plans to some of my friends so that, in case of emergency, they would know where to search for me. I had to do some explaining to the Military Police guard at the campus gate as to why I was leaving on foot at such an early hour on a very frosty Sunday morning.

I descended the steep street putting the military base behind me and was soon walking through the silent darkness of the village streets. The peace was only disturbed by the occasional bark of a dog or the squall of a startled alley-cat. I strolled quietly along the narrow winding cobble stone streets and soon crossed the wooden foot bridge spanning the river. A wide path led from the far end of the bridge into the inky black pine forest.

I had dressed warmly and was beginning to be too warm as a result of the brisk walk to that point. Based upon past experiences climbing German mountains during chilly weather, I intentionally over-dressed. My plan was to shed clothing when it became uncomfortable, hide it, and recover it upon my return.

I followed the path for approximately a mile before waiting for daylight, in order that I may find a suitable spot to begin my climb. A large over-hanging cliff appeared in the dim pre-dawn light very much resembling the entrance to a cave. Upon closer examination with a flashlight, I discovered a large oil painting with a gilded frame sheltered from the weather and mounted to the wall of the over-hanging cliff. That did not surprise me, for Germans frequently express their admiration of art and nature at such locations. The paintings usually have a religious connotation. Typically, there also was a nice wooden park bench opposite the path where hikers could rest and enjoy the painting.

It would be too much trouble attempting to eat breakfast after beginning my climb, so I sat upon the bench and waited for more daylight. With breakfast behind me, I found a place to hide my heavy clothing. A half mile beyond the bench, I found a well-worn access route up the back side of the mountain. It was steep, but did not require special climbing gear. I could make rather fast progress, in spite of a dense fog which seemed to ooze from the forest floor and restricted vision to just a few feet. By the time I had climbed half way up the peak, I had hidden all of my clothing , except shoes, trousers, and a sweat-shirt.

After an hour, I reached the lower edge of the bare granite spire above which no vegetation grew. Prior to arriving at that point, I had doubts that I would be able to climb the bare rock without partners and special equipment, but I was surprised that someone had installed and anchored a steel cable to assist climbers. By holding to it, I could walk almost upright the remaining distance to the summit. I had risen above the fog and had broken into brilliant morning sunlight.

I was surprised once more upon reaching the summit and viewed at close range the cross I could barely see from the valley floor. Instead of being small, it was at least ten feet tall. The wooden tim-bers, from which it was made, were almost one foot square and the upright portion was held in place without bracing, because the base was inserted into a hole chiseled into the solid granite. I estimated that those timbers weighed hundreds of pounds and was amazed at the brute effort that must have been required to drag them up the side of that steep mountain.

Having reached the top, I sat upon the rock and held myself in place by crooking an arm around the upright of the cross. At first, the valley was blanketed by the dense fog. Only the mountain peaks of the Alps were visible to the horizon in all directions. After an hour or so, the sun began dispersing the fog and I could look directly down at the red tile roofs of Oberammergau, which means Upper Ammer

Valley. Within another hour, the fog completely disappeared, affording me a wider view including the neighboring village of Unterammergau, which means Lower Ammer Valley. I felt almost entranced as I inhaled the pristine fresh air and slowly munched my remaining food, while simultaneously absorbing that magnificent view from my lofty perch.

Some time later, I was shaken out of my day-dream by voices coming from the trail below me. Two young German lovers came into view holding the cable. I made room for them on the limited space available as we talked for a while. It was not long before other climbers approached the summit, making it too crowded for me to remain there. I had accomplished what I came for, so I departed in order that others could enjoy what had been an exhilarating experience for me. As I descended the peak, I met many other people on their way up. We chatted cheerfully and moved on. I recovered my hidden clothing, after which I spent the afternoon strolling the beautiful pathways surrounding the base of Der Korper. I shall always cherish the memory of that beautiful day. I returned to campus in time to eat dinner at the mess-hall with my friends.

From that day onward, I could look across the valley at Der Korper as a Friend rather than some mysterious stranger to be conquered. I like to think that the spirit of Der Korper also remembers me as a loving Friend.

Operation Nordic Air

It was early January 1965 in Germany. I was a paratrooper with the US Army's Eighth Infantry Division and was the Station Chief of a counter-intelligence detachment at the Rhine River city of Mainz. One morning, I received a telephone call directing me to spend three weeks with a maneuver planning group at Division Headquarters twenty miles away at Bad Kreuznach. Our task was to write plans for an airborne war-game to take place in June near the town of Boris, located on the North Sea costal plain of Denmark.

Our First Airborne Brigade was to oppose the Queen's Scottish Fusilier Brigade from England, allied with the Denmark Home Guard. My section of the planning committee consisted of three other men charged with developing an effective counter-intelligence plan. Assessment reports made available to us stated that the Fusiliers were a formidable, well-trained fighting force, whose history was replete with decorations for skill and bravery. After all, they were the Queen of England's favorite military unit. On the other hand, the Danes are some of the world's most non-warlike people. They do not excel in military science and tactics. Most of their army is comprised of home guard troops, who wear military uniforms a few days per month, but live at home and have regular jobs. As a member of the North Atlantic Treaty Organization (NATO), Denmark is expected to contribute troops in the event of a general war in Europe. The Danish Government thought that a joint maneuver on Danish soil would be valuable training for their soldiers in defense of their home soil.

From the start, my team thought that the Danes would be no match for our paratroopers, but, since the Scots would be under their command, we didn't think that either force would be much of a threat. Besides, the Scots, just as ourselves, would be unfamiliar with the maneuver area. As allies of the Danes, they would be taking control of highways, railways, radio/TV stations, or newspapers. We were also informed that they would debark and take positions surrounding our drop zone. For the most part, they would also be facing a language barrier, thus, limiting coordination between they and the Danes.

The NATO Command, which issued the rules regulating the war game, directed that our paratroopers would be the Enemy invasion force, and that we would be surrounded on all sides outnumbered ten to one. Well, we assumed that would be fair odds, because paratroopers are usually dropped behind enemy lines and are outnumbered. It was NATO's plan that we would be over-ran and forced to surrender. We recognized that we have some advantages from the start. We would be fighting back to back in a compact group with concentrated fire-power in all directions, would be well dug-in, and, although we had many multi-linguists among us, we only had to communicate with each other without language barriers in English.

We paratroopers were not accustomed to losing. We did not care what the NATO Brass had planned, if we saw an opening, we were going to try to win. At least, we were not going to make it easy for any force that had us outnumbered ten to one. So my little team had to dream up a very effective plan. We knew that the maneuver would begin with a mass parachute assault at mid-night of June 21. We also knew that on June 1st each year, all teachers at American military installations throughout Europe were given their summer vacations, with a choice of either returning to America, or to tour Europe. Many elected to remain in Europe, visiting other nations each summer, including Denmark. Danish people were accustomed to seeing them. So, ah ha! There was our opening into Denmark's defense; we would recruit a couple of the school teachers to operate behind enemy lines. We would meet and debrief them when we arrived at the 'staging-area' at Tristrup Air Base, Denmark.

They reported that the plan began working like a well-oiled machine from the start. What a vacation! They were eating wonderful Danish food, meeting equally wonderful people, and especially friendly Danish soldiers, who were thrilled that Americans would come such a long distance to see them perform their duties as soldiers. They took our teachers to their clubs, their barracks, and on tours of Camp Boris. They could not believe that they were trusted so much. They avoided meeting any Danish officers, who may become suspicious and have them arrested, so they targeted low-ranking enlisted men who were usually young and boastful. They were anxious to demonstrate how important they were.

We learned that the most officers and senior sergeants lived in town, leaving the military bases in the care of duty personnel at night and on week-ends. Since they did not anticipate any emergency, discipline was lax. We learned that, if an emergency did occur, the soldiers living in town, would drive their personal cars to the scene. That became helpful to know a few days later, for when the alarm sounded for the maneuver to begin, hundreds of cars were driven and parked at the vast area surrounding our drop zone. Any captured American need only have someone distract their guards, hot-wire a car, and drive it through friendly lines, for anything is fair in war.

The weather had been glorious throughout our visit to Denmark and lasted the day-light hours and through midnight when the maneuver was scheduled to start. We were in high spirits as we donned our parachutes near five o'clock and hundreds of men began boarding the giant C-130 planes preparatory to our jump at mid-night. It was a moonless night, but we had learned during our time in Denmark, that being so far North, the sun makes its usual flight across the day-time sky, but, rather than setting out of view, it just barely hides behind the northern horizon at night. One could easily see well enough to read a newspaper on such a clear night. It requires much time to load, launch, and format dozens of planes for a mass air assault, so we flew at random for almost four hours before reaching the drop zone on schedule.

Standing near the open door as we approached the drop-zone, I could see numerous flashes of blank enemy ground-fire lighting the inside of the plane. The C-130 planes were flying wing-tip to wing-tip in huge V-formations both in front of and behind the one I was riding. US Air Force fighter planes were zooming and diving at enemy positions around the edges of the drop-zone in mock strafing runs. The roar was deafening. Suddenly, the red light came on signaling that we were twenty seconds before jump time. The troopers were yelling go! go! go! as I threw my static line toward the rear of the plane and heard it zing along the steel anchor-line. I pivoted and leaped out the door, brought my feet together, tucked my elbows tight against my sides, and pressed my chin against my chest awaiting that brutal opening shock to come. The blast from the two turbo-prop engines on that side of the plane, wafted me like a feather as I heard blood making ticking sounds in my ears, and then came the bone-shattering tug as the chute filled with air informing me that I had made one more successful jump. Suddenly, the sky was full of parachutes containing both men and the chutes of many five hundred pound bundles of equipment, which the pilots released from the bombay hatch at the front of the planes, while men exited the back doors. The air was really crowded and I had to be alert for falling objects. That hazard was repeated every time wave after wave of planes dropped their loads.

It required less than two minutes for me and my one hundred ten pound load to reach the ground with a thump. The ground was covered by a thick tangle of waist deep heather, upon which I tripped as my ankles sank into the soft damp sand of the North Sea coast. There was no ground wind to fight my chute, which collapsed over me like a tent, but when I fell, one hip came into painful contact with something hard on the ground. Thinking it was a grenade or a pistol that some trooper had lost while aloft, I groped in the sand and discovered what I had struck. I was holding a stone that was both round and slender, about five inches long. It was hard and smooth. A good souvenir, I thought as I dropped it into my pack. Over the next four days, I discovered that there was no stone in the area. Upon later examination of the stone I had found, I observed that it had been grooved and notched for a handle. It also had one large chip, as though it had impacted something with force. I have kept it on my desk until present and am convinced that it is a Nordic war hammer, possibly a relic of an ancient battle.

The drop-zone was approximately three miles wide by five miles long. In the twilight, the hundreds of men straining to walk through the dense heather with their bulky packs resembled herds of buffalo. My Unit's assembly plan was for those who were the first to jump to follow the plane's line of flight toward the center of the drop-zone and those who jumped last to retrace the plane's line of flight toward the center. That way we would all meet near the designated area of the combat zone, where Brigade Headquarters would set up operations. Each Unit had pre-designated areas of the drop-zone. They were to assemble and move outward until making contact with the enemy.

Everything went as planned. Except for the continued assault by the fighter planes, the sky was quiet now. The constant roar of ground-fire and explosives was more constant now that combat troops on each side confronted the other. Parachute injuries were very few, except for one trooper who was killed, having fallen upon high-tension electric wires. As we set about our business, a cold breeze began to blow in from the North Sea. Just as suddenly, a dense fog seemed to literally roll across the ground, reducing visibility to zero, followed by torrents of icy rain. When daylight arrived, visibility was still not more than fifty feet. As it happened, the fog and rain did not end for the next four days and three nights. There was nothing growing upon that treeless plain with which to build a fire. We paratroopers had only the clothing and food with which we jumped. We were supposed to be re-supplied by air every morning of the maneuver, but the weather prevented the planes from flying.

Every step taken through the water-laden heather sent it streaming down our legs into our sodden boots. The ponchos we wore did an adequate job of keeping our upper bodies dry. We hadn't anticipated forty degree weather in mid-June, so most of our heavy clothing remained in Germany. I had experienced situations like this before, so I ate only after I could endure hunger no longer. Even then, I disciplined myself to eat only two ounces of meat and beans and two crackers at six o'clock morning and six o'clock evening. For one thing, there was no scarcity of water.

Paratroopers are accustomed to being miserable and enduring hardship. We had a war to win and could not allow ourselves to forget that. We knew the Danes had very little stomach for that kind of adversity. We were supposed to lose the war, but to the consternation of the NATO umpires, our troopers were expanding our 'beach-head' in all directions and were capturing Danes by the hundreds. The Scots were much tougher, however, but they were being left defenseless, when many of the Danes on their flanks deserted en mass and simply went home. So we had our hands full of fuming Scots cursing the 'spineless' Danes. The umpires were enraged.

Winning the engagement took our minds off our discomfort to some degree, but nothing lifted our morale like the success of a plan that I helped devise with my five-man team. We informed the Brigade Commander of the layout inside the Danish Army base. Also, upon debriefing some of our escaped troopers, we were informed that due to the bad weather, Danish officers would close their command post at eleven o'clock at night and go to bed; and that many enlisted men simply took refuge inside their private cars parked nearby. The Danish Commanding General slept inside his mobile war-room, a large van body mounted upon a truck. Some of our men had been taken there as prisoners to be interrogated and they had observed a padlock hanging open on its hasp by the only access door to the van.

Our plan to end the war with victory was to dress a few of our troopers in Danish Army uniforms, equip them with captured Danish rifles, and let them herd a hundred of our men through the porous lines toward the compound gate near mid-night, pretending that Danish soldiers had captured them.

The plan was put into action. When the Danish guards saw the throng approaching, they assumed that their comrades had scored a big success and threw the gate wide open. Before the guards realized their mistake, the Americans broke formation, rushed through the gate, and captured the guards. Once inside the base, our commandos silenced power generators, cut telephone lines, stuck 'destroyed' signs on water towers, fuel tanks, and the ammunition dump. Upon reaching the Commanding General's van, they snapped the open lock shut with him inside. A driver started the engine and led the way with the horn blasting, as their fellow marauders stole any other vehicles they could find, and raced out the gate en route to our Brigade Headquarters.

The next morning the rain stopped, the clouds lifted, and the sun came out bright and warm. The sun was not the only thing that was warm. There was a gaggle of roaring NATO umpires demanding to know why we had won, a Danish General with cheeks rosy from embarrassment, and hoards of Scots demanding the heads of every Dane upon a platter. Simply put --we won.

Oh yes. My souvenir still makes me smile.

Christopher Columbus's Birth Place

While stationed with the 11th Airborne Division at Augsburg, Germany during 1957, my family consisting of my wife, son, daughter, and I made a twenty-one day camping tour of Italy. We traveled 'light', carrying a tent and other necessary camping equipment in the trunk of our car. The first leg of our trip led across Southern Bavaria through Garmisch-Partenkirchen near the German-Austrian border, where we soon reached Innsbruck, Austria, famous as a former site of Winter Olympics. From the lofty mountain road we traveled, Innsbruck at its base appeared to be the size of a postage stamp. The road, with many dozens of u-turns, spiraled through some of the World's most breath-taking scenery. We spent part of the sunny afternoon visiting a ski-jump and other points of interest, before traveling once more up the steep mountain through Brenner Pass into Italy.

At that time, we were paying twenty eight cents per gallon for gasoline on military bases, while most Europeans were paying at least four dollars per gallon in their countries. There was sufficient gasoline in our tank to reach an airbase occupied by the United States Air Force at Avianno. At that location, we purchased a coupon book of gasoline stamps at twenty eight cents per gallon, sufficient to last until returning to Germany at the end of our tour. We also found a suitable camp-ground by a lake, where we spent the first night of our camping trip. My children were swimming in the tepid water at daybreak. They were intrigued upon encountering night fishermen bringing their boats ashore.

It was an easy trip from Avianno to Venice, where we spent our entire second day. We arrived at a parking lot adjacent to Marco Polo's ancient headquarters building from which he embarked upon and returned from his trek to China. It was also the location of a vast gondola boarding station. We hired a small one capable of carrying our small family and directed the Gondolier to take us on a tour of the city, which included a visit to a glass factory, the Bridge of Sighs, a visit to the famous harbor filled with many ships of the world, and finally a landing at the huge Saints Marks Cathedral.

Aside from being the largest structure in Venice, measuring 220 feet wide and 250 feet long, Saint Mark's is one of the most ornate and beautiful buildings on earth. It is considered the civic center of Venice, being located at the far extremity of a paved frontal plaza approximately three hundred yards long and one hundred fifty yards wide. A choice of five huge ornate portals topped by exterior walls of white, blue, red, brown, and gold lead to the cathedral's jeweled interior, whose dome is forty five feet in diameter. The exterior roof is adorned by numerous small spires and domes.

The arched Bridge of Sighs extends across a canal, one end attached to a court house, the other end attached to a former dungeon. The covered arched bridge is gracefully designed, with windows lining the lengths of both of its walls. The name of the bridge had its origin during ancient days when prisoners were sentenced to life in the dungeon never to see daylight again. As they were lead across the bridge to the dungeon, it is told their deep sighs could be heard. As a note of interest, a duplicate of the Bridge Of Sighs can be seen as an above-street cross-walk between two buildings at Pittsburgh, Pennsylvania.

Our wonderful day ended with our nine year old son, wearing the Gondolier's hat, and standing upon the gondola platform helping the gondolier to row. The setting sun glowed upon our five year old daughter's face as she appeared to be entranced by the Gondolier's magnificent tenor voice as he sang an Italian song.

Early the next morning, we were visiting Bologna, the city whose sidewalks throughout its business center are covered by porch-like roofs of buildings. Access to the buildings is via ten foot wide curb-side archways called arcades. Another feature we found fascinating, were two large towers shaped like, but shorter than, the Washington Monument. They poked fun at the Leaning Tower of Pisa with the premise, if Pisa could have a tower that leaned accidentally, Bologna could have one by design. One tower was built standing vertical, while the other was built beside it leaning approximately ten degrees.

A trip through the Apennines Mountains, which resemble a spine slanting from north-west to south-east mid-way across Italy, is an experience to remember in that most highways across them follow the ridge-lines. A distant building or other land-mark may not appear to be upon the route being traveled, but eventually the traveler finds himself passing by it at roadside. That feature can really frustrate a traveler in a hurry to make forward progress. Another feature of that region harks back to ancient times, when travelers on foot or riding animals in caravans did so in groups for precaution against bandit attacks. The drab sparsely populated walled villages consist mostly of adobe-like castles, ancient inns, narrow streets, clustered apartment buildings, and a few individual houses. They served as 'way-side inns' spaced one day's foot travel apart to accommodate caravans en route from Italy's cities to those such as Paris in central Europe. Except for modern automobiles, time and amenities in those villages appears to have stood still. Farming techniques are also primitive in that most of the steep infertile agricultural land consists of vast ancient terraces extending from mountain tops to the valleys below. The tan landscape is almost treeless and is boring to behold.

It was refreshing to finally leave the Apennines behind and to arrive at the beautiful, musical, and artistic city of Florence. I remember seeing a picture of an ancient covered bridge across the Arno River named the Ponte Vecchio in my fourth grade geography book during 1931. The sides appeared to be made of warped unpainted barn-boards at that early time of my life. I was amazed to find it still existing when we actually saw it. It continued to appear unchanged after having survived the rigors of World War II and the ravages of many winters. It is not used for vehicular travel, but rather, for many curio shops and foot traffic.

Upon leaving Florence, we traveled to Rome, where we rented a space at a 'secured' international camp-ground atop one of the city's seven hills providing a panoramic view of the entire city. We spent two days at that camp-ground, while touring the Vatican, Saint Peters Cathedral, Saint John's in The Lateran, Saint Paul's Outside the Walls (the site where Paul was beheaded), the Parthenon with its open dome, Victor Emmanuel's Tomb (the last king of Italy), The Fountain De Trivia, The Mannequin Piz, the former seat of the Roman Government called The Forum, the under-ground cemetery named the Catacombs, and The Coliseum.

On a Sunday during our visit, we were among an estimated one hundred thousand people gathered at Saint Peter's Square to see a Mass by Pope Pius. He was carried seated upon a platform by a dozen men who passed within a few yards from where we stood. Later, we visited inside Saint Peter's Cathedral, which was so awesome it defied description.

A visit to the caves of the seemingly endless catacombs was the definition of eerie. At the entrance, a monk provides each tourist with a short length of twine string, which has been dipped in wax to form a tiny candle. When lit, it was hoped that it would prevent a person from becoming lost from the crowd. Since the monk conducted visits every day, his candle was continuous and loosely looped around his forearm. The catacombs are not natural caves, but are a maze of tunnels excavated from the soft subsurface beneath the city where persecuted Christians hid from Roman authorities. As residents died, the survivors carved shelved along the walls of the caves, wrapped the deceased inside layers of cloth, and laid the corpses unburied upon the open shelves. The small candles were capable of lasting for less than an hour. Tourists viewing the dead as they passed through the tunnels, were careful not become separated from the others.

A visit to the Coliseum depicts the cruel history of the Roman Empire. It is huge, measuring six hundred feet long by five hundred ten feet wide by one hundred fifty seven feet high, and has at least two levels of basement. During its early days, it could seat forty five thousand people. The original floors were wooden. There were cages installed around the base of the wall at ground floor level to hold fierce jungle cats and bears. As entertainment for Roman spectators, the savage animals were released to attack families of Christians, who tried to defend themselves with only their hands. Holding-cells to house slaves and gladiators were located in the basement areas.

There was a time when all of the exterior walls of major government buildings in Rome were covered by marble or granite. Those materials could only be obtained from quarries in the Alps of northern Italy and dragged to Rome by oxen with great difficulty. Each new Caesar considered himself superior in every way to those whom he followed to power, so he contemptuously stripped marble and granite from his predecessor's buildings to construct his own. That has resulted in many previous buildings being left in ruins. There are plans to identify and use heads, bodies, legs, and arms of many dozens of former statues which are strewn about the 'forum area', where they previously adorned magnificent buildings and court-yards. The most prominent ruin still identifiable is the stage where Mark Antony made his memorable remark, "We have not come to praise Caesar, but to bury him." The Coliseum would have been completely destroyed were it not for Pope Benedict XIV ordering its preservation during 1700 AD. Other than being a tourist attraction, it is currently famous as the home of stray cats. Since the greatest emphasis impressed upon tourists visiting Rome is upon its ancient history, we departed with a sensation that we were leaving a cemetery.

Once we began traveling south of Rome and seeing the beautiful coastal towns and beaches along the Mediterranean Sea, our children dressed only in their swimsuits. July days in southern Italy are hot, so they took many quick dips into the water. We arrived at the major harbor city of Naples where many US Navy ships pay frequent visits. Anticipating a return trip through Naples, we proceeded onward to Pompeii, where we planned to climb the live volcano, Mount Vesuvius. Although it was in plain view, without exact knowledge of a road to reach that destination, we hired a guide. Our car was large compared to those of Italy, but we were ill prepared to make room for a guide who weighed a minimum of three hundred pounds! My wife joined the children in the back seat. Our car had a pronounced list as that huge man crowded into the passenger space, and his 'over-flow' seriously encroached into my own driving space.

As is true of most Italian mountain roads, the narrow steaming hot one leading to the summit was comprised by a chain of u-turns. Near the top of the mountain, we arrived at a small vineyard village which had a single-lane one-way street going upward and another going downward. Typical of the very argument-prone Italians, just as we reached the junction of the two streets, a truck driver entered the wrong way on the one we were on. He refused to simply back and go the proper way. The windows of the many storied buildings aflutter with laundry lines were also occupied head and shoulders by dozens of shouting housewives, who had nothing better to do than enter the argument. After a long delay, a policeman arrived and entered the verbal fray, which caused us to sit in that sweltering heat for at least forty minutes.

Upon finally arriving at the volcano, we were greeted by a scientist operating a seismograph. He related that, since the last devastating eruption in 1944 during World War II, causing four armies to back away for weeks, the site is manned twenty fours daily in hopes of providing sufficient advanced warning so the population for many miles could evacuate in advance of another eruption. That and previous eruptions had twice buried the city of Pompeii. After seeing a constant three foot high flame licking through a crack only a few yards from where the man was seated, we were a bit reluctant to accept his invitation to walk approximately two hundred yards and enter the open crater left by the 1944 eruption. To make certain that tourists were convinced that the flame is real, he maintained a stack of newspapers and was using them to light their cigarettes. Already near roasting from the baking sun and the hot ground, we spent a few minutes inside the crater. From that lofty point, we could see the storied island of Capri beyond the harbor of Naples.

On our return trip through the village, we were gratified that the street was not blocked by another 'lunk-head'. The immediate problem was worrying if our brakes would get to hot to prevent us from crashing. I kept the car in low gear and used the brakes as sparingly as possible. With the extra load of our guide, I truly worried as I kept close watch of approaching runaway ramps near each turn. It did not become necessary to use them, but if I had, we would have had plenty of Italian associates, whose brakes were cooling as they parked in the emergency ramps. It was great relief to have that giant out of our car once more upon reaching the bottom of the mountain.

After cooling ourselves with some refreshments, we made a foot tour of sections of the ancient buried city of Pompeii. Although the excavation had been in progress for many years by 1957 when we were there, the task was far from being complete. It was such a vast step back in time to look into iron-gated court-yards of houses occupied by former Roman families. Near sundown that day, we watched an Italian motion picture company filming a scene in that enchanting place.

We located an international camp-ground nearby, where we spent the night. It had been a hot and tiring day, so we retired soon after eating our evening meal. I was sleeping soundly when little Sue awakened me. She said, "Daddy, something is biting me."

I turned on a light and could hardly believe my eyes. Her skin had numerous red welts as large as the ends of my thumbs. Our son was also tossing restlessly, so I aroused him. I discovered that he, too, suffered many bites. That was when I was amazed to see dozens of white snails coating every surface inside our tent, bedding, and equipment. There was no way we could continue to sleep inside the tent. After treating the children's bites with liniment, we took sleeping bags, pillows and blankets to our car, after removing all snails from them. Since our children were small, we made beds on the back seat and the rear floor, while my wife and I slept sitting on the front seat. It took an hour after daybreak to clear our tent, bedding, and equipment of snails. We feared that some terrible malady would befall the children, but no further damage to them occurred. The undersurface of our car was coated by snails. Most of them dislodged on our return trip to Germany, but to attest to their power of adhesion, we returned to America during 1959, remained in America an additional year, was transferred to Korea for three years, and when my car was on a lift in preparation to ship it back home, I still found dead Italian snail shells continuing to cling to under-surfaces and fenders of our car.

The following morning, we went to the Naples pier so the children could look at the ships. To our surprise, among vendors wares for sale at a market located there, numerous bushel baskets were filled with white snails like the ones inside our tent. Thousands of them had crawled out of the baskets and solidly coated their exterior surfaces. That was when we discovered for the first time that Italians love to eat snails. For the time remaining on our vacation, we were cautious to avoid any food product which could possibly contain any part of a snail. Yuk!

We began our return trip leaving Naples and making the long drive to Pisa. Traveling along the scenic Mediterranean coast was treat to remember. At least once every two hours, our children spied a pretty little beach and we would take a swim to relieve the scorching heat.

Upon seeing Pisa, I was surprised to discover that the leaning tower does not stand alone. In addition to it there is a cluster of other ornate buildings including a church built of the same type of stone and architectural design. Naively, I had always assumed that only the leaning tower occupied the site, and could not comprehend its purpose. We did not spend much time there, since our allotted days of vacation were waning.

My son was anxious to see Columbus's birthplace located at Genoa. We found a pleasant beach where we could camp after leaving Pisa. Back on the road early the next day near eleven o'clock, we reached Genoa. The harbor is surrounded by some low hills near the northern tip of the Apennines Mountains. Upon driving into the central business district after visiting the famous harbor, I was fortunate to find a commercial parking lot. Upon arrival, I saw two parking attendants parking the tiny telephone booth sized Italian cars of that era by pushing them like one would a shopping cart. I pulled onto the lot and exited our car. I have no training in the Italian Language, but I was rather certain that many words were similar to Spanish of which I had slight knowledge. When they approached me, I paid the parking fee and gave them the key to the ignition.

After they returned my key, I mustered my best attempt to communicate our wishes by saying, " Pardonname Signore, donda est las Casa de Colombo?"

"Ah Colombo!" They both shouted at the same instant.

One of them grasped my elbow and escorted me across the street adjacent to the parking lot and enthusiastically pointed to the small vine covered stone house at the foot of the hill bordering the next street. We walked the short distance and stood in awe that such a simple abode was the birth-place of perhaps Italy's most famous explorer. We mused that from such inauspicious beginnings, many of the World's most renowned persons made their indelible contribution to History. As is natural, I took measure of myself, and wondered if

I ever had the courage to do what Columbus had done. I advised my children of how privileged they were among millions of American school children to be standing at that hallowed place.

My admiration for that great benefactor swelled in my breast and dwelt upon my mind throughout the afternoon as we traveled toward Milan. I tried to imagine a youth no older than my nine year old son frequently visiting the wharfs of Genoa's harbor to mingle with and listen to the seamen who sailed the costal oceans during that age of early exploration. No doubt he listened to many theories concerning the nature of the earth and the Universe in general. He must have heard the superstitious arguments that the world is flat as others would counter with the belief that it is round. Although he was not considered a scientist, he must have formulated his own opinion that the world is round through logic. For instance, if the moon and stars are round, why not the earth? If the earth is flat, why does the sun disappear in the West each evening and reappear in the East each morning? If one observes the ease with which water rapidly flows downgrade, why do the oceans not empty themselves by flowing over the edge of the earth into outer space? As he grew to adulthood and went to sea in coastal waters, he must have observed ships disappear beyond the horizon, but later return safely to shore. When far to sea with no land in sight, he must have observed that the horizon is formed like an arc, not flat, although the water, itself, is level. When another ship appears from beneath the horizon and not visible here-to-fore, where did it come from? Did it appear from beneath the water or was it invisible below the curvature of the earth?

Columbus may not have been a scientist, but if he were alive today, I have little doubt that he would be an enthusiastic participant in the explorations of outer space. His life history is one of foresight, courage, bravery, accomplishment, hardship, combat , and ship wreck. He also suffered disappointment, betrayal, envy, resentment, abandonment, and unearned disgrace at the hands of competitors and fickle monarchs.

Having reached and passed through Milan, we made camp at beautiful Lake Como. We lost a bit of our enthusiasm for swimming after taking a quick evening dip into the glacier-fed waters of that lake. The night air also became crisp, influenced by the run-off of distant snow-covered peaks among the Alps.

The resumption of our homeward trip the following morning through the narrow pool-table green valleys of northern Italy with their quaint rustic houses built of stone and stained wood was a feast of indescribable beauty. As the valley floor gained altitude, we crossed the border into Switzerland where we climbed the exceptionally steep narrow serpentine highway through St. Gothard Pass and Tunnel. Upon clearing them, we found ourselves viewing the head-waters of the mighty Rhine River. No poet, artist, or silver-tongued orator could adequately describe the beauty of that part of the earth.

I hasten to admit, until we arrived at its border, I never knew that Liechtenstein, Europe's fourth smallest nation, existed. There it stands located on the Eastern bank of the Rhine River, containing sixty one square miles (near the size of Washington, D.C.), and land-locked between Austria and Switzerland. Its government is a Constitutional Monarchy governed by a fifteen member Diet. The population is approximately 14,000 and its language is German. It has no Army. It must be one of the most peaceful places on earth.

Our next camp-site was at Zurich, Switzerland on a bluff overlooking the city and Lake Zurich. The beauty of that spot was mired for us by the only rain storm of our entire trip. Sheets of blinding frigid rain lasted an entire day and night, dampening our equipment and our spirits. The next morning, we packed our car with our soggy belongings and traveled through improving weather to Lake Constance on the German-Swiss border. Warm sunshine arrived once more by mid-day, so we made camp on the lake shore. The warm afternoon temperature allowed us to string clothes-lines and thoroughly dry our equipment before night-fall. It was there that we enjoyed a much better night of rest before making the relatively short trip home northward through southern Bavaria to Augsburg.

A Bleak Christmas

Three days after Christmas 1961, the temperature was four degrees above zero Fahrenheit with a bitter cold wind blowing off the South China Sea. It was before daylight at the mouth of the Imjin River located near the western extremity the North/South Demilitarized Zone (DMZ). We four members of the US Embassy's Army Attache Office at Seoul had driven in an ancient Jeep station-wagon approximately thirty miles to that location over a rough rutted unpaved road typical of those found in the countryside of South Korea. We often traveled to that area, a South Korean Army out-post, to hunt ducks and pheasants, so we timed our arrival hoping to be in duck-blinds before daybreak.

Due to the harshness of winter, as well as the isolation of that dismal spot, with no availability of any sources of food, lodging, or service stations, we always dressed warmly, carried tools, extra gas, spare tires, and surplus food to cover emergencies. Favorite food items easy to carry were hard-boiled eggs, sandwiches, thermoses of coffee, hot chocolate, dried fruit, potted meats, candy bars, and oranges. Since we were in the Army always prepared for an emergency, we also carried a full case of combat field rations.

In order to reach our destination, it was necessary to leave the road and drive two miles atop a high earthen dyke installed to protect the tens of thousands of acres of rice fields from the South China Sea's thirty-two foot twice daily tide, one of the highest on Earth. Always before, there were sentries posted at the compound's gate, but not that morning. With hostile North Korean troops within sight upon the high ground just beyond the DMZ, that was unthinkable. Being Americans and traveling in a vehicle bearing Diplomatic License Plates, the Koreans always accorded us immediate access to the out-post.

Each member of our party had visited that location many pervious times, so our arrival was a familiar sight. The out-post was a miserable primitive place during the best of times. It was comprised of six canvas squad tents, several fortified sand bagged bunkers, some fifty caliber machine gun emplacements, and a few dozen fifty-five gallon oil drums normally used to store fuel oil, but now empty and scattered about lying on their sides.

During daylight hours, the camouflaged North Korean bunkers and facilities were faintly visible in the distance. In order to harass the South Korean soldiers and attempt to deprive them of sleep, beginning at dark each day and lasting until daylight, the North Koreans used high-powered loud speakers to play the World's weirdest non-melodic music alternated with screaming Communist propaganda.

My friends and I were accustomed to seeing the stark conditions under which the Korean soldiers lived, but none were prepared to witness what was taking place that morning. As our vehicle entered the compound, our lights revealed three platoons of approximately forty men each standing in rank at rigid attention without either headdress or gloves, and with their bodies naked to their waists. The three platoon sergeants were likewise standing before their platoons. Only a lieutenant in charge was warmly dressed.

We Americans were enraged, but we realized that, being guests in their country, there was no way we could interfere. It would cause an international incident. As we dismounted our vehicle, amazement showing upon our faces, the lieutenant sensed that we should be given an explanation for such a brutal display. Without as much as a glance toward his troops, he approached us and spoke in English.

He told us that the outpost was normally commanded by a Major, who had a Jeep and driver for his convenience. The outpost was also assigned one two and one half ton cargo truck for transportation of supplies. He said the Unit was normally re-supplied all of its needs near the first of each month, but for some unknown reason, they received only half of what should have received for December. In spite of careful rationing, they ran out of both food and heating oil the week before Christmas.

The Major had received many invitations to Christmas and New Year parties at Seoul. As was customary for higher ranking officers, they spent at least a week each year in high society. The Major was fully aware that his troops had no supplies, so he had the supply truck to follow him to Seoul. He either neglected to make the proper arrangements for supplies, or the truck crew decided that they, too, would enjoy the Christmas season in the big city.

But, why was the Lieutenant punishing his men, we asked.

He replied that every man there was dedicated to give his life rather than fail his duty defending his country against the North Koreans. To desert their post was unthinkable. Near starvation, he discovered that some of the men had deserted their post at night to visit local villages to beg for food. Due to his fatalistic devotion to duty and with fear that he, himself, would face courts martial and prison, he forbade anyone to abandon the compound for any reason. He, therefore, was punishing everyone to make certain that he included the ones who had violated his order.

We had no idea how that situation was resolved, nor how much longer those men were required to stand there. Each of we four had served many years in our own army. At times, we had undergone incidents of great misery, but nothing to compare to that. We decided to donate the ducks we shot that day to the starving men. That, however, may have been perceived as an insult, because Koreans considered ducks as dirty and did not normally eat them. Perhaps, under the circumstances, they may have been a welcomed meal. We also donated all of our meager food supply, cigarette lighters, matches, spare gasoline, and the case of combat rations to the starving men. Near ten o'clock when the flocks of ducks no longer appeared, we returned to the compound, the men were no longer standing in formation, we were greeted by the strained smiles of many haggard grateful men.

The following morning, we informed the Korean Military Liaison Officer, whose duty station was at our Embassy, about what we had observed. I have no doubt that harsh action was taken to correct both the supply and command problem at the Korean out-post.

Christmas 1926

The day before Christmas at the orphanage was like every other day at the orphanage. Awakened at six o'clock, dress, be marched to the basement toilet with dozens of other boys, wash faces and hands, march to breakfast at the dining room on the ground floor. Eat oatmeal as thick as tar, eat clumpy scrambled eggs, bacon so salty one's tongue felt like it was shrinking, and toast as hard as a shingle. No talking. Eat every bite or get whacked. March back to the toilet to brush teeth. March to the second floor playroom to await permission to play. Yep, the day before Christmas at the orphanage was like every other day at the orphanage.

Why was the little boy living at such a place? Not by choice, that was certain, but he was fortunate to have a place to live at all. His Mother was dead and his father had abandoned him. To save him from starvation, State Social Workers sent him to live at the orphanage. It wasn't home, but he had a roof over his head, a cot to sleep on, and food to eat. He, along with the other boys and girls, was fortunate to be living there, because many people were having a hard time trying to survive

That was the little boy's first year at the orphanage. His life there was neither happy nor easy. He was skinny, pale, and undernourished. He and the other children spent the boring days wishing that they were a part of a loving family. Each wished to be adopted. Since most days were dreary and unhappy, the little boy learned not to expect much from life. He often wondered if it would not have been better if he had died like his Mother had. What would become of him? Was he so unimportant that he was given away like an animal and was sent to a shelter? Should he try to survive now that he had been launched into life by his parents? Could he actually survive being unloved, unknown, and unwanted? What would become of him without a family? How long could he endure his present mirthless boring existence at an orphanage where he was treated more like a thing than a human?

From the first day of his arrival and he was herded into the boy's crowded playroom, crying and bewildered, he was comforted by another little boy named Charlie. While all the other boys stared at him without showing any sympathy, Charlie stepped forward, placed his arm around the newcomer's shoulder and said, "Don't be afraid, I'll be your friend." From that day onward, Charlie became the little boy's family, confidant, and friend. They became inseparable. If they were awake, they were together. Without Charlie's friendship, the little boy would have gone insane.

So, it was the night before Christmas. The children were never told by their handlers what was going to happen from day to day. They were just told to line up for this or that, then herded along. It came as nor surprise, when after dark, the children were told to form a line in a hallway outside a room which the little boy had never entered. He could only remember one Christmas, when he was younger. He did not understand much about it.

After a while, the line began to move through the tall doorway which opened into a large assembly room on the ground floor. It was as dark as mid-night inside that room. As soon as the last child was inside and the door was closed, someone turned on the lights. Dozens of little eyes gazed in wonder at a huge Christmas tree, which must have been ten feet tall. Many of the children had never seen a Christmas tree. What a sight to behold. Just by its being there, it filled the room with its spicy aroma. Most of the little voices said "Ah-h-h!" as the lights caused the decorated tree to shimmer and come to life. As the children hopped about with delight, the breeze they generated caused the branches to wave gently up and down. The tree was decorated with great fluffy ropes of tinsel, popcorn strung on twine, imitation icicles made of strips of silver colored foil, and sparkling baubles of many sizes, shapes, and colors. Underneath the tree were piles of fluffy white cotton in folds and peaks to resemble drifting snow. Perched at the top of the tree was a small white angel doll.

The room, itself, had been lavishly decorated for the occasion. A huge red tissue paper bell hung from the center of the ceiling. Affixed to it and sagging gracefully and extending to each corner of the high ceiling were gently twisted ribbons of red and green crape paper. Evenly spaced the length of each ribbon were tiny silver colored sleigh-bells, which fluttered and tingled merrily with each breeze created by the opening or closing of a door. Large green wreathes sprinkled with glitter and also containing sprigs of holly containing bright red berries hung from the center of large windows along the outside wall of the room. That scene held the children in a moment of open mouthed enchantment.

Suddenly, a tall door opened to outside as a great gust of cold air rushed into the room. The silver bells tingled and the Christmas tree waved its branches as there for all to see, stood an enormous man with snow-white hair and whiskers. He was dressed in a bright red suit trimmed with white fur. He also wore a matching red hat also trimmed by white fur and topped by a white tassel. He wore a shiny black belt with matching boots. He rang a small bell, which he held in his right hand, while his left hand grasped the top of a large canvas bag draped across his shoulder. He voiced a booming ho ho ho as he bounced into the room looking like a huge red fur-ball riding atop a pogo-stick. His continued ho ho hos through his smiling lips seemed to come from deep inside a volcano, as he patted each child on the head en route to a chair placed beside the Christmas tree. There he dropped his bag and began holding hands with the children, as they danced about the room. His was the first smiling adult face that most of the children had seen since coming to the orphanage. For a short while their troubles were forgotten and their sad hearts were gladdened.

After dancing with the children for several minutes, Santa plopped heavily onto the chair and opened his sack. As their names were called, to each little girl he gave a paper bag containing some fruit, candy, and nuts including a tiny baby doll. Also calling each boy's, he also gave a mixed bag of goodies in addition a little red aluminum fire-truck. The children hugged Santa and thanked him for their gifts, before gathering in groups with their friends to share their newly kindled happiness. Santa rose to his feet, waved a Merry

Christmas to all and ho hoed his way into the night as quickly as he had arrived.

But Santa had not called Charlie's little friend's name. He had learned from the past experiences of sadness not to expect much from life, but being overlooked that night nearly crushed his heart. He tried to be brave and not allow that wave of sadness to overwhelm him. After all, he reasoned, had he not had a good time? Had he not forgotten his troubles? Also, were his friends having a good time? He decided to do nothing which would lessen the joy they were having. Quietly, he retreated into the dark shadows at the edge of the room behind the Christmas tree. He sat on the floor with his legs extended and feet together. He leaned his back against the wall, folded his arms across his chest, and stared at his feet. He tried to shut the activities in the room from his mind, but he was having difficulty holding back tears. His lower lip tooted out as he bit his upper lip trying not to cry. He could not help feeling forgotten and alone.

He was not forgotten. Just as other children sought their closest friends with whom to share the fun, Charlie Greathouse was trying to find him. Charlie finally found him where he sat upon the floor.

Charlie rushed to his friend's side and exclaimed, "Hey, look what I've got!"

Then Charlie stopped short. "What did you get? Why are you hiding in the dark?"

The little boy was so close to tears that he blurted, "Nothing." Then he hugged Charlie and burst into tears.

Charlie tried to comfort his friend and said, "This is awful. I'm going to tell Mrs. Harshbarger."

He located the house matron and told her about his friend being omitted from the gift list. Fortunately, someone had prepared for such an event. A few extra packages had been placed beneath the Christmas tree. Thanks to good friend Charlie, he and several other of their friends gathered around the sad little boy as Mrs. Harshbarger presented him a gift package. They all cheered as he opened his package. Inside was a little red aluminum fire truck.

As always happens, winter is followed by summer. Little fire-trucks, as do most toys, eventually wear out from use, but they do not become valueless to little boys, who love to hide buried treasures.

After helping all of the boys to lessen the long winter boredom of being confined indoors for weeks at a time, the separate parts of the little fire-trucks were tenderly stored in tin cans and were buried at secret locations along the orphanage's boundary fences and beneath huge Norwegian pine trees growing throughout the large lawn. Since aluminum does not decay, the treasure of Charlie and his little friend lies where it was buried eighty years ago as of this writing.

Edward Gets To Keep His Name

When I became an orphan at a very young age, the only possession I had upon arriving at the orphans' home was my name, James
Edward Martin. The reason I was there was because my Mother
had died. My Father, who for reasons never known by me, disappeared and abandoned me. I had no grandparents, brothers, sisters,
or other relative to whom I could turn to for love, comfort, shelter,
or safety.

There is never a good time to become an orphan. Each day, I
read or hear of many husbands and wives who have broken their
wedding vows and became divorced. I have always been taught
that my word is my bond. That is, if I make a promise, it is sacred
and I am expected keep it. The saddest aspect of divorce is that they
often occur after one or more children have been born in the family,
thus, destroying their world. The family structure of having both a
mother and a father is no longer intact. Children are always the ones
who suffer most. They find themselves being passed back and forth
between their mother and father, their grandparents, foster homes,
or to orphanages; whatever becomes convenient for the adults. The
convenience of the children becomes unimportant to their parents.
Often divorces are followed by remarriages resulting in more passing children about as they become merged into another family as
strangers to a step-parent and to other children with whom they must
share a home.

Of course, there are those who become orphans because of some
tragedy. Sisters and brothers are often separated adding to their
unhappiness. In the bewildering struggle to survive, children ask,
"Who am I? Why has my world gone crazy?" They feel unwanted

and they finally come to the realization that they are going to spend their lives among strangers and their only remaining possession is their name.

I had been a resident of The West Virginia Orphan Home, Elkins, West Virginia for three years when, on a sunny afternoon during June 1929, my best friend, Charlie Greathouse and I were passing another day of boredom by swatting flies upon the concrete steps leading into the dining hall, when we were summoned to the Superintendent's office. We looked at each other with wonderment, knowing from past experience that only for punishment was one called to that office. We had learned to stay out of sight and never to attract attention, because orphans were often beaten as punishment for things we had not done. Charlie and I were wondering what we were going to be accused of this time, for we had not done anything wrong. With fear and apprehension, we crept into the office. Standing just inside the room was a frail little orphan girl whom we only knew as Mary. To our surprise, in addition to the Superintendent, his wife, and the wicked old house-matron, was a pleasant looking elderly gray haired woman and a man dressed in a chauffeur's uniform. The Superintendent, his wife, and the matron were beaming with the most uncharacteristic smiles as though they were the kindest people on earth. They addressed we children in the most honeyed tones and related to the strange lady, Mrs. Smith, that we were three of the orphanage's most loved and greatest treasures. I could not help but wonder if Mrs. Smith could see the red welts on my legs caused by a recent beating by Mrs. Harshbarger's switches.

She cooed we children to go to our bathrooms to bathe and return wearing the new clothing waiting there for us, because we were being adopted. All three of us sounded a war-whoop of joy as Charlie and I raced down the stairs to the boys' bathroom were we had undergone torture, been scalded, and almost drowned by being held under the surface of soapy water by the older boys . In addition, we were scratched raw by being scrubbed with stiff-bristled brushes every Saturday night since our arrival. This was the first time in my life when I was allowed to give myself a bath. We wasted no time dressing into the dark blue Navy-styled linen suits with short sleeves and pants. It was summertime, so it did not surprise me that we were not given shoes to wear. I did not own the clothing, nor was I leaving with a tooth brush or a comb. I was leaving the orphan home with no more than with which I had arrived --my name.

I was certain that I was dreaming when we walked through the front doorway of that awful place for the last time. We three children climbed onto the back seat of a large black Studebaker touring car with high disc wheels. Dozens of children lined the driveway waving goodbye as the car passed between the tall brick gate-posts and entered the town streets. Within a few minutes, we were leaving town on a southbound dusty country road which is called US 219/92 today.

The late afternoon wore on as we children chatted excitedly about the sights which were new to us. I occasionally pinched myself to be certain that I was not dreaming. Could I be free at last? Eventually, the sun set behind high mountains, as we left Route 92 at Huntersville and was now traveling solely upon Route 219 toward Marlinton, leaving the lovely valley behind.

Earlier during the afternoon when there was light by which Mrs. Smith could read each child's record, I recall hearing her speak to Mr. Morgan, the chauffeur, "What a pity that Edward is going to have his last name changed." She continued by saying that he is going to live with a family in Virginia (whose name I cannot remember) and Charlie is going to a family named Martin.

"When I get to Lewisburg , " she said, "I'm going to get permission to switch their destinations, because neither family has seen either boy they will get. That way, only Charlie will have to change his name."

I felt like hugging her. I should tell you, adopting a child was much less formal during those days of economic 'hard times' of the 'Great Depression'. If a family wanted a child, they simply ordered it by contacting a Social Worker. I know for a fact, the Martins were wanting a strong boy who could perform farm labor. They said "Send me a boy." I was thus a 'mail-order boy much like bachelors of old would order a bride. Actually, I was never adopted by the Martins. I became what is known as a 'foster child.'

Darkness arrived as passed through the little village of Slaty Fork and began climbing lofty Elk Mountain. We children were enchanted by the way shadows played at the edges of the car's light beams. Once atop Elk, the bright stars in the moonless sky seemed almost close enough to touch. After years inside the orphanage, we had never seen such a treat. Soon, we could also see the distant lights of Marlinton glittering in the valley far below. We were greatly excited in that wild new world of enchantment.

Arriving at Marlinton, we were still forty miles from Lewisburg, so Mrs. Smith stopped at a hotel for the night. I had never been to a hotel and had not eaten in a restaurant. The adventure of this trip was one I would never forget. My imagination was running wild, for I was in a world I never dreamed existed. Sights that are so commonplace to me today, held me in absolute awe. Above everything else, I was amazed that I once more could engage in childish laughter and feel the excitement of inward joy, which had died within me during those gruesome mirthless days at the orphanage.

We finished our trip to Lewisburg the following morning, where a new sadness crept into our lives. Although we had a happy trip the day before, each of us knew that we would be having to say goodbye the following day. Parting was especially sad for Charlie and I, because he had been my best friend from the day I arrived at the orphanage three years earlier. He was the first person to place his arm around my shoulder when I was crying. He said, "Eddie, I will be your friend." I have not seen Charlie and Mary again. There was no way for us to stay in touch, because none of knew where we were going.

As for me, my new life was by no means easy, but it was much better than living at the orphanage. I learned several years later how old I was after getting a Birth Certificate and that I was eight years old when I arrived at my new home. I had only been taught the alphabet, how to count to ten, and to write my name. I was older and behind my classmates when I started to school. Most of them could read the stories of Baby Ray and Dick and Jane. I caught up quickly and was promoted twice one year.

When I entered high-school, I met a beautiful brown-eyed girl named Betty Jean Martin. We fell in love and, after returning home from World War II, Betty Jean and I were married. That wedding sixty years ago to that Martin girl of my dreams made me even more proud of my name. How could I be so fortunate? I have gone from owning only one thing to being given a most wonderful treasure, a lifetime with the girl I love who also shares my name.

Nary a Ghost in the Night

Many years ago, children living in our West Virginia farm community would sit quietly upon a floor and listen intently to every word of stories being told by the old folk. Adults during those days thought children should be seen, not heard. They expected children to be polite, when in the presence of adults, and not to speak unless spoken to.

Children really wanted to be quiet and listen when neighbors came to spend a few hours of conversation, because they knew it would eventually turn to stories about the old days about heroes, battles, and hardship. Some stories were about major storms, floods, and fires. Others were about great horses, heroic dogs, and men's great feats of strength and bravery. Prize fights of 'boxing greats' such as John L. Sullivan, Gene Tunny, and Jack Dempsey were often described. Usually, someone would relate tales of ghosts and haunted houses. Some of the most thrilling tales would be about panthers and mountain lions, whose shrill squalls sounded like babies crying, would cause chills to race up and down the children's spines. Sometimes, there were stories about giant eagles who snatched children from play-grounds, carrying them away never to be seen again. And how about marauding bears so huge they killed grown horses, cattle, and sometimes broke into cabins at night destroying entire families.

Of course, these enhanced wild tales were told as being the absolute truth. Some of the most chilling were told about snow-white ghosts floating slowly about some of the local cemeteries on dark nights and voicing eerie o-o-ohs. Others told of old abandoned houses rotting down in disrepair where dim lights flickered behind curtains of spider webs so vast they waved from glassless windows at night. They were said to be places where stray cats made their homes living by consuming bats and rats. The doors and shutters barely hanging from rusted hinges, emitted eerie screeching sounds as they were banged open and shut by the wind. Those stories were scary enough to make a child cringe with fear, but I wouldn't have willingly missed a minute of it.

I never did fully believe those stories, but I thrilled at hearing them. I accepted the possibility that the animal stories were logical, but I had suspicion that they were greatly exaggerated. West Virginia mountains are forested and vast. It is no secret that bears and an occasional mountain lion do exist there and they can pose a real danger.

Many of my chores on the farm had to be done after the evening meal at the end of a long work-day. I always prided myself for not being afraid of the dark. I was very young at the time and had never faced the necessity of making a journey alone on foot any distance from the farmstead at night.

My foster father was addicted to tobacco. He became a grinch when he expended his supply. He owned a truck, which he could have driven to a store, but one night he roared, "I'm out of tobacco. You take a hen from the chicken house and go to the store," he commanded me. My heart sank as I envisioned the two mile trip during which I would have to walk through dense forests existing at that time and also enter one deep hollow. I carried a kerosene lantern to light my way and it would surely scare away wild animals, but I would pass a cemetery mentioned during story-telling events describing ghosts seen there. In addition, I would pass within yards of a vacant house also said to be haunted. Finally, I would have to walk beneath a tree reputed to have been the lynching site of two run-away slaves during the Civil War. I heard it said that on still dark nights, the spirits of those two men could be heard moaning.

I tried to be brave as I wondered if I had the courage to make that trip. I was feeling great anger surging within myself, when I thought of the lazy man causing me to do what he should be doing. He was the one who wanted tobacco, not I. A genuine fear prevented me from defying that six foot two hundred twenty pound man, so I mustered my courage and chose the lesser of two dangers. I decided that, since

I could not refuse to go, I was determined to prove or disprove those stories for myself. I reasoned that, if they were true, they may scare me, but nothing about them could harm me.

As I approached the cemetery, I paused to watch and listen. There was no difference than the many times I had passed it during the light of day. Likewise, with the cemetery behind me, I paused before the vacant house without hearing or seeing anything. By far, the most unnerving ordeal lay ahead of me. As I topped the hill upon which the massive hang-man's tree stood, I could see its massive shape dimly outlined against the sky. I held the lantern high to illuminate the tree as I crept with trepidation one slow step, paused, and stepped again until I stood directly below the over-hanging limb. Nothing. Absolute silence. I began to doubt that any part of that story was true.

I felt a great burden escape my mind and body. I was truly exhilarated as I felt that I had proven I had courage.

Having closed his store ending the business day at nine o'clock, my foster uncle was preparing to go to bed, when I knocked upon his door. When he opened his door and saw me standing there with a lantern in one hand and a chicken in the other he said, "Lad, what are you here for at this time of night?"

I answered him by saying, "Dad is out of tobacco. He sent me for a can of Prince Albert and two books of cigarette papers" as I handed him the chicken.

He mumbled something uncomplimentary under his breath about his brother-in-law's stupid tobacco habit as he snatched the chicken and the lantern from my hands and went to his own chicken-house. He returned and obtained the tobacco from inside his store.

My return up the steep mountain road was uneventful. Upon my return, the impatient tobacco fiend literally snatched the tobacco from my hand and grumbled about why it had taken me so long. I had become accustomed to having my feelings hurt, but nothing could suppress the enormous pride that swelled my chest. I have lived a long time since that night having visited many parts of the World and have learned that there are many animals capable of doing me bodily harm, but there is one thing for certain -- there are no (nary) ghosts in the night.

Milking Time on the Farm

There was a time in our Country when people were less depen-
dent upon markets than upon themselves. Life as a sort of 'cottage
industry', can be described as making or growing almost everything
a person needs by engaging in agriculture upon a farm. Before the
end of the horse and carriage days, and in many cases even after the
introduction of automobiles. houses located inside large cities had
picket fences around their lots. In the back yard next to an alley,
there would be a stable and carriage house, a small shed for a cow
and a pig, a coop for a few chickens, and a vegetable garden plot.
The same pattern existed in small towns and villages, but on a much
larger scale upon farms.

Prior to the development of streetcars, doctors, merchants, and
office workers living in cities and towns traveled to their places of
business by carriages drawn by fleet-footed high-stepping horses. As
more easy methods of travel developed in urban areas, supermarkets
were established at points of easy access. Patients began going to
doctor's offices, instead of the doctor coming to their homes. Farm
animals, back-yard barns, stables, and gardens began to disappear
from urban neighborhoods. Even the method of hand-milking cows
was replaced by milking machines.

As a farm boy, my chores included carrying firewood and coal
into our house, filling the water buckets at the well-pump for house-
hold use, feeding cows, horses, pigs, sheep, chickens, dogs, and cats,
and milking cows by hand. Long after life in the cities had modern-
ized, folk living on farms continued to live much the same as they
had for hundreds of years, although cars became a common sight in
the countryside. Aside from large dairy farms with hundreds of cows,

most families living on small farms had only two or three to provide milk, cheese, and butter.

Our family was so poor, we seldom traveled more than a few miles from our farm and we never stayed away from home overnight. There was one thing certain, the farm chores had to be done morning and night every day of the year. There was no circumstance which would change that, even if a family member died. The chores mentioned above were often assigned to the farm children by the time they reached   six or seven years old. As the oldest of two boys, it became my job to do the chores until my brother, who was nine years younger than I, became large enough to help.

My day always began while the sky was still dark. During winter months, I always kindled the fires; thawed the ice in the water buckets which had frozen solid atop the kitchen table; fed the cats and dogs, then , with a kerosene lantern and buckets, went to the barn to feed the other animals. By the time I finished my chores, including milking two cows, breakfast was hot and steamy in my Mother's kitchen.

It is, however, about milking cows morning and night that I relate this story. Milking cows was the most time-consuming and least popular chore on the farm. Everybody I ever knew just hated milking cows. Oh sure, some old daisy-eaters became such pampered family pets, I am surprised that their doting owners didn't take them into bed with themselves. But, let me tell you, cattle left to their own desires are just plain unclean creatures. They wade right into the water ponds where they muddy or otherwise contaminate it for themselves and the other cattle. Regardless of how much clean dry bedding is provided, they manage to soil their bodies each night. They trample through their forage always searching for something more tasty, thus rendering the feed they have just dirtied inedible for themselves and their neighbors. Turn them loose in a lush green pasture and they will find some filth to lie in, even on bright sunny days. In the interest of sanitation, even during freezing weather, it was absolutely necessary to bathe the entire area surrounding the udder of each cow prior to milking. Even under the best of circumstances, that became quite a problem.

All of the farm animals knew when it was feeding time. They would approach me and impatiently urge me to dispense their food. We had from four to six cats at various times who seldom strayed from the barn where they could find plenty of mice and where they could burrow deep warm beds beneath the mounds of hay in the barn loft. They also knew when it was milking time, for I always poured milk for them to drink into bowls I placed at the barn for that purpose. The cats always became impatient to be fed, but they mustered as much etiquette of which they were capable by perching atop the wide base sill along the barn foundation. They would sit side by side facing me a few feet away where I sat upon a three-legged milking stool. The only fun I associated with the milking chore came when I would hold one of the cow's teats in my hand, squeeze it hard, and aim a steam of warm milk at each cat's face. The milk would strike each cat with a splat. It was hilarious to watch as I moved the stream from cat to cat, then move back to the first one for another pass. They sat rigidly working their mouths and sticking out their tongues with the rhythm of a piano teacher's metronome. With the regularity of the sunrise and sunset, the cats waited for me to take my undignified position upon the milking stool while reaching under the cow with both hands to perform my duties. The cats would later spend a long time grooming themselves to remove the milk from their fur.

I am certain that those nostalgic days of hand milking cows have passed into history's dust bin, just as have the carriage house, the one-horse buggy, and those quaint little houses we sometimes referred to as 'outside plumbing'. In order to obtain the milk you desire, it is improbable that any who read this story will ever suffer the indignity of having a spiteful cow give you a hot milk bath by kicking the bucket, or getting whopped on the side of your head with a frozen filthy ice-caked or cockle-bur laden hammer-like tail .

I recall times when I would be milking on one side of a cow, while her baby calf would be nursing on the other side. I would perform my task like a cultured gentleman, but for the life of me, I could never understand why an impatient greedy calf wolfing down torrents of milk, would butt its mother's udder with the force of a boxer's uppercut. It must have translated into a complaint that the cow was not providing the milk fast enough to please the calf. Another thing I could not understand was, instead of kicking the whey out of the offending calf, without failure, the cow would kick me in retaliation. I could never predict when the impulse to butt would seize the calf, but when it happened, the sequence of the cow's lightning-fast triple reaction was the hammer blow by her tail, followed by a kick, and then came the milk bath. But, I was just a dumb ole farm boy, who was told that was the way it was supposed to be done. I can see it in your eyes right now; you are itching to ask me, "Why didn't you simply rob the cow of your half of the milk and then turn the pesky calf in afterward to do its thing?" Well, you see, that is the value of an education and I can see that solution clearly now. I also am pleased that you are receiving that education without having it literally pounded into your head by a tail blow to your head.

I'll close this story by relating another that closely resembles mine. It was told that a very wicked farmer had the reputation of using the foulest language of anyone else in his community. He finally listened earnestly to the pleadings of his family and neighbors to go to church and change his ways. Just as I began and ended my farm days contending with cows and their calves, the one event which ignited that farmer's wrath more than anything else was when a calf hunched the cow, the cow would hit his head with her sodden tail, and she would kick the bucket.

Part of the farmer's new obligation was his promise to go to church every Sunday night. So it happened. He dressed in his blue serge Sunday suit and went to the barn to milk the cow. Just as I did before becoming educated, he began milking with the calf on one side and he on the other. Everything was happening just fine. He was sitting upon his stool holding a teat in each hand. He was squeezing out steady streams of milk into the bucket with skill. The calf was extracting huge gulps of milk like a one hundred fifty pound suction pump. The farmer was feeling so pleased with his new conception of life and was humming the tune of 'The Old Rugged Cross'. He was confident that nothing unpleasant was going to happen to him since he had made a new covenant with his Maker when WHAM! With lightning speed, the calf unleashed an uppercut that almost lifted the cow off her feet. You guessed it. That cow swung her 'Louisville slugger' tail to the side of the farmer's head, she kicked the bucket, and the blue serge suit now looked like a milk dud.

Once more the farmer felt the return of that old-time feeling. He wiped the milk dripping from his eyebrows with the sleeve of his coat, dashed to the other side of the cow, and grasped the calf's tail as one would hold a well-pump handle. While yanking the tail up and down with all of his might, he struggled to suppress his frustration and mustered more self-control than he had ever known to keep from using foul language. Gritting his teeth and almost popping a button off his shirt collar in livid rage he shouted, "If it was not for my dad-burned religion, I'd kick the living stuffing out of you!"

There you have it. Just be thankful that, when you want a glass of milk, you can have it by going to the refrigerator. You won't have to work for it and, what is more, you shouldn't have to fight for it.

The Schoolteacher with No Legs

I was a resident at an orphanage. One day, a West Virginia family provided me a foster home where I grew to adulthood. I soon discovered that I was a member of a large family of aunts, uncles, and cousins. One of those was my foster Mother's brother, Burnice, who never married and occasionally lived with us. I remember the first time I saw him. Although he was a young adult, he was quite small and had to use crutches to walk. That was because both of his legs were withered and under-developed. I could tell by the ease with which he moved that he had been using crutches for a long time. In fact, when he was only a few years old, he became the victim of spinal meningitis, which he survived, but the disease crippled both legs.

At the time I first saw him, he had graduated from college with a teaching degree and was attending Marshall University to attain a Masters Degree. That was during 1929, when the United States was entering an economic crisis known as 'The Great Depression.' Money was almost non-existent and it was almost impossible to get a paying job, especially for a man with crippled legs.

Burnice was very optimistic, however, because he believed that he could overcome any obstacle. He had a cheerful outlook and an abiding confidence in himself. When not at college, he spent a few weeks with first one then another of his sisters' families, because he did not own a home. The passage of time was not kind to him, however, for by the time he completed his Master's Degree, the constricted blood vessels in his withered legs began causing great pain. His feet were becoming infected to the stage where doctors warned him that gangrene was almost certain to take his life. The only solution was to have both of his legs amputated above his knees.

I can remember how bravely he accepted his plight the day he boarded a train with his father en route to Johns Hopkins Hospital in Maryland. The next time I saw him, he continued to use crutches, but he now was wearing two life-sized artificial legs. He never became able to walk without crutches.

He came to live at our house for approximately a year, while toughening his stumps and becoming accustomed to wearing the artificial legs. During that year, I became both a close friend and helper. He had a pleasing personality and a keen wit. His excellent education and love of children was a great treasure to me and my own developing mind.

Burnice realized that he needed mobility if he hoped to obtain a job and become independent. From newspapers, he learned the West Virginia State Government at Charleston planned to conduct an auction of confiscated automobiles formerly belonging to people convicted of transporting and marketing illegal whiskey. Most of the vehicles were of good quality and capable of high speed. One brother-in-law and another driver accompanied Burnice to the auction, where, fortunately for him, he bought a Model-A Ford coupe with a rumble seat. Through inquiry, the men located an automotive shop, which specialized in equipping cars with special controls for handycaped people. The men returned to our farm with Burnice and his car. Burnice spent several days inside one of our meadows developing driving skills. When he was certain he could pass the driving test, he did so easily. Now, he was ready to find a job.

As you may imagine, there were few elementary schools in Greenbrier County being taught by teachers with Master Degrees. Burnice became one, but when he applied for a teaching position, members of the Board of Education expressed little enthusiasm for hiring a teacher on crutches. Although qualified to do so, they flatly refused to hire him as a high-school teacher. They also knew the severity of West Virginia winters and doubted his ability to drive a car through the mud and ruts of Greenbrier County's terrible dirt wagon roads under the best of circumstances. Burnice was persuasive, however, and willing to demonstrate he could drive as well, if not better than most of the Board Members. He may have had a bit of political clout, since his Father had been Superintendent of Greenbrier County Schools a few years previously and was the current principal of Smoot High School. Burnice requested and was assigned to the one-room Brown Elementary School located three quarters of a mile from our home. He could teach at Brown and continue to live with our family.

If you find the definition of courage in a dictionary, Burnice's picture should be displayed beside it. That man had more 'grit' than any person I have known. You have heard that, "when the going gets tough, the tough get going." I have witnessed that, when that road became almost impassable for cars, it was a tiresome adventure to travel it on foot. It also frequently became impassible by almost any means, when drifted almost six feet deep with snow. I have been with Burnice when his car would stall. He and I would lie in the mud and dripping water beneath the car and install wheel chains to get it restarted. There were times during the two years he taught at Brown when it was necessary for my foster father to take Burnice to and from school on horseback, because of deep snow.

One of the voiced concerns of the Board of Education was, how could a legless man maintain discipline? Near the mid-point of his first year at Brown, a wicked man, who had recently been released from prison, moved his family into a vacant farm-house in our neighborhood. Gentle folk, who spent their entire lives in that vicinity, were deeply disturbed that a man of that nature was now living among them. He had two sons, whom he enrolled at Brown. Each of the brothers weighed approximately one hundred eighty pounds, although only twelve and fourteen years of age. The oldest was in seventh grade and the younger in sixth.

The brothers immediately began acting like bullies and did everything possible to disrupt classes. Burnice had to schedule class times carefully, because he had students in all grades from first through eighth. The bully brothers thought that they could take advantage of Burnice's handycap to do anything that pleased them. They refused to accept any instruction and would not perform assignments. Burnice wrote a letter of complaint to their father, asking him to make his sons conduct themselves properly, but the oldest brother tore the letter to bits and flung the pieces at Burnice's face. After another half day attempting to reason with them, Burnice expelled them and sent them home at mid-day.

Before classes began the following morning, Burnice, a few other early arrivals, and I were standing upon the school porch, that level of which was attained by climbing seven wooden steps. We saw the nasty man and his sons approaching the school. The father was carrying a wooden pick handle and walked at a fast pace. He appeared to be angry. There was a savage snarl surrounding his yellow teeth, as he approached the porch steps.

He did not accord Burnice the courtesy of calling him Mister as he growled, "Haynes, my boys tell me that you won't let them come back to school."

"That is right," answered Burnice. "They refuse to comply with my rules of conduct, so I expelled them."

While vigorously shaking the pick handle at Burnice in a threatening manner, the furious man shouted, "Yer gonna takem back! Thar's nobuddy gonna expel my younguns, especially not a puny cripple that ought not be tryin tuh teach school in the first place! Now ya say yer gonna take em back or ahm gonna teach ya a lesson with this pick handle ya won't fergit!"

That said, he started to climb the steps with his sons close behind him.

Burnice remained where he was leaning against the porch banisters and, in a calm voice steady voice, said, "Sir, I am crippled, but I am not puny. If you climb those steps, I will crush your skull with this crutch. I have the authority to expel your sons and I will not take them back. If you wish to try me, just come up here."

The other students and I showed support by flanking and backing Burnice, trying to appear as menacing as possible, but I am certain it was the fire in his eyes that stopped that man in his tracks. He backed away from the steps and growled to his sons, "Let's go."

The man could not resist hurling a final threat, after he had taken only a few steps, turned, and once more pointed the pick handle at Burnice.

"Jist watch yer back, Haynes," he threatened. "Ya won't always have school property to protect ya. Me an my boys will be seein ya around."

I did not see either the man or his sons again, because it did not take that family long to make enemies of all of their neighbors. Shunned, they moved away as suddenly as they had arrived and were never heard of again.

Burnice developed an interest in County politics, so he did not seek continued assignments as a teacher. He was elected as a Justice of the Peace with an office at Rainelle, West Virginia. People who hold that position at present are called Magistrates. He established his office in one half of a store-front building on Rainelle's Main Street. There was an additional room and a toilet behind his business office which became his living quarters.

Within a few months, Burnice's ancient grandfather, who lived at Corless, became gravely ill and lingered near death for several weeks. It was necessary for someone to attend his bedside needs twenty-four hours each day. People available to provide such care were few, so, after performing his office duties each day, Burnice would take turns staying several hours a night at the old man's bedside. Nearly exhausted, Burnice returned to his quarters late one night. He had developed a fondness for smoking cigars and could be seen during most of his working hours with one in his mouth. You may imagine how helpless he would be in the event of an emergency, after removing his artificial legs and laying his crutches aside when going to bed. The Fire Chief said that he must have fallen asleep with a lighted cigar in his mouth.

The building was a total loss and my wonderful Friend was gone forever.

Blind Russ

This story had its beginning inside a West Virginia coal mine during the year of 1921. The hero's name was Russell Mitchell, whose family and friends called Russ. He was an intelligent and carefree sixteen year old lad, six feet tall, and weighing a muscular one hundred ninety pounds. Since he was 'under-age', in order to get his first job, Russ requested that his coal mining father, George Mitchell, obtain a work permit for him at the mines.

It was sad that Russ's mining career did not last long. One day, he was preparing to make a 'shot'. It was necessary for a miner, through the use of a long hand-cranked steel augur, to drill a 'shot hole' into the base of the undisturbed wall of coal in order to loosen enough coal to be shoveled into a coal car. Following that, a stick of dynamite had to be prepared for shooting by pushing a large nail into one of its ends, making a hole large enough to insert a brass-cased primer-cap the diameter and appearance of a rifle cartridge into it. The primer cap also had to be prepared by inserting the end of a coil of blasting fuse-cord into it. The procedure was simple, for once the fuse cord was inserted, the miner used a small pair of pliers to crimp the thin end of the brass primer case enough to prevent the fuse-cord from falling out. Once all of that had been accomplished, a wooden stick, such as a broom handle, was used to push the dynamite into the auger-hole. To prevent the dynamite stick from accidentally becoming dislodged, a ball of mud was inserted and tamped snuggly into the hole.

Just as Russ was preparing to crimp the primer cap, a drop of flaming oil leaked from the miner-lamp mounted upon the front of his helmet and splashed upon the primer. Fortunately the primer had not been inserted into the dynamite, for the resulting explosion would have killed both he and his father. Unfortunately, however, the flaming oil ignited the powder-laden primer he was holding. The resulting explosion showered Russ with bits of brass, instantly blinding both of his eyes.

His accident would have ended the working career of many less resolute men, but not Russ. For certain, he suffered pain and felt sorry for himself for a short time. Anyone would have. His family and friends gave him sympathy and support, but Russ was not one to allow adversity to overpower him. His Father blamed himself for having gotten his son a job in the mine, one of the most dangerous occupations in the 'working-world'. In fact, many of George's friends believed that his overwhelming grief because of the accident, accelerating the rapid decline in his own health. He entered deep depression resulting in a paralytic stroke rendering him bed-fast for twenty six years until he died.

Russ knew that pity could not restore his sight. Common sense told him that his life had to go on. He learned of a school for the blind located at Romney, West Virginia where he could learn to read specially prepared manuscripts and books written in a substitute alphabet, which used raised dots on paper over which the student could learn to read by sliding fingertips over them. The system of letters, numbers, and punctuation marks is called Braille. Attending that school meant that Russ would have to acquire a completely new education, but he gladly accepted the challenge, for at the Romney School, a student could study the arts, literature, mathematics, music, language, business management, and crafts. Russ elected to master two paths to qualify himself to be self-supporting. He completed the business management course in addition to learning how to manufacture house-hold brooms.

Russ was interested in returning to his home community where he could enter business. Following graduation, that was what he did. He was already operating his business the first time I met him. Until he generated enough income to afford a house of his own, he returned to his parents' farm, where he was born. I discovered that his family was our nearest neighbors upon my arrival during June 1929 from the West Virginia Orphan Home at Elkins, West Virginia.

Russ was a hero to all children living in our neighborhood, not because he was blind, but because he was a genuinely good person, just as were his Father, George, and his Mother Maggie Mitchell. Big handsome jolly Russ had a smile which could light a dark room. He truly was a person whom people would go out of their way to be with.

Until he could earn enough money to lease a business location at Rainelle, West Virginia, Russ made brooms at home. He sold them upon the streets of Rainelle, where he developed trust and many more friendships. Other business owners were interested in helping Russ succeed, so they approached him with the idea of installing a soft-drink and snack shop along the side-walk adjacent to the Alpine Theater. The shop would not need to be large; a mere food stand, which would attract theater-goers during evenings and Saturday afternoons. The merchants furnished the building materials for the drop-front stand, carpenters contributed their labor, and the town provided the small plot of land for the non-permanent building rent-free. Food and beverage companies extended Russ credit, which he could pay back from profits. A minimum hook-up of water and electricity, for which he could also pay from profits, completed the tiny business installation.

Within a short time, Russ was happily greeting friends and selling drinks, candy bars, and pop-corn. During those early days of radio, motion picture theaters did a thriving business almost every day and night. Russ became widely known and was greatly admired, so his little business also thrived. It was always a great treat for me to visit his stand on Saturday nights en route to the movies. The wonderful smells of pop-corn, brewed coffee, and hot-dogs could be smelled a block away, wafted by the evening breeze. That message sent by my nose to my brain set this farm boy's mouth to watering.

One thing which always amazed me was how Russ could rec- ognize who someone was by merely hearing the voice. There were times when I would see Russ infrequently, but the instant I spoke, Russ would say, "Hello Ed". I was not an isolated case, however, for I have observed customer after customer approach and speak to Russ and he would call their names. It is said that blind people develop a keen sensitivity to their surroundings by improving their remaining senses of touch, hearing, taste, and smell. Also great powers of memory.

After becoming successful, Russ was fortunate to locate and purchase a small house within two blocks from his business. He could easily walk upon the level sidewalk without having to cross a busy street, except for one quiet intersection. A few years after entering business, Russ met and married a well educated lady who was blind from birth. She did not attend a special school until after graduating from high school. She had attended both elementary and high school with children who could see. She earned passing grades by listening closely to what was being taught and she prepared her home-work in cooperation with her friends, who would read to her. Later, Watha graduated from a school for the blind at Cincinnati, Ohio and another at Columbus, Ohio.

Watha shared the operation of business with Russ and brought a new joy to his life. Together, they had two healthy daughters, whose ability to see made their parents' lives much less complicated. It is easy to imagine that those little girls played some childish pranks upon their parents at times.

With the invention of television as well as the creation of drive-in theaters, the Alpine Theater at Rainelle closed. Russ also had to close his little stand. A few years later, Russ died. News of his passing saddened thousands of people who knew him. He had been a Legend; a living role model to those who experienced great hardship. Those unwilling to quit when the mere process of living seemed almost too difficult to endure could think of Russ and take new hope. His success in business afforded him a comfortable living and provision for his widow and children after he was gone. In the town of Rainelle, there are no statues in memory of its citizens, but those of us who still remember Russ, he is a monument of splendor in our memories.

Thus ends the story of that handsome young man whose eyes once viewed the verdant green mountains of West Virginia, who spent the majority of his life in darkness as deep as the inside of that long-abandoned mine where this story began. Both Russ and that mine have been reunited beneath the soil of this earth.

The Country Stores

The country stores that were located at thousands of rural cross-roads throughout the United States during your grandparents lives are treated like relics or small museums today. They are rapidly disappearing from the American scene, but many are being restored as tourist attractions. Although touted as monuments of our Nation's earlier history, so many modern things have been installed in and around them, they are often a poor imitation. It is almost impossible to find an unchanged one today. You children would hear some interesting and entertaining stories if you would ask your grandparents to tell about the country stores they knew when they were young.

The typical country store was a square warehouse type two-story wooden building of simple design with a gable roof. Most had a full-width porch, had a wide front door, and two large double-sash front windows on the ground floor. Small side windows were usually placed high near the eves of the roof so as not to interfere with interior merchandise shelves and usable wall space. Most storage and warehouse rooms were attached to either side or the rear of the main building in the form of a lean-to shed.

Most country stores were built next to their owners' residences, but some merchants lived on upper floors above their businesses. During the time of their prominence, the stores were usually found where two roads intersected and generally they were spaced conveniently only a few miles apart so that rural customers could easily walk, ride horses, or travel by horse-drawn vehicles to reach them. Each country store, many of which also contained a Post Office, became the activity center of the community which they served. It became commonplace to also locate the churches and schools near them.

To create a secure place to house the Post Office, the merchant, who usually also became the Postmaster, would build a small room which could be locked inside a front corner of the store. A steel bar-grid-work and a metal cabinet containing a few dozen 'pigeon hole' letter boxes with brass doors and combination locks formed the front wall of the Post Office. Those private boxes were rented to patrons who walked to the facility each day. People in the countryside had their mail delivered to private boxes at their houses.

Life in and around a country store was the happiest place in a community with quartets singing four-part harmony; the presence of story-tellers, tobacco chewers, whittlers, knife traders, and horse-shoe pitchers. Women would congregate to discuss the art of quilting and to pass a wee bit of gossip. The merchants, themselves, seldom became rich, but they and their families enjoyed an easy life. I cannot recall ever knowing an unpleasant country merchant. In fact, most of them were the best liked people in a community. It just seemed that they were always in a jolly state of mind. When someone entered the door and the merchant said, "Good morning!" It sounded as though he really meant it.

As the community social centers, the front porches were usually equipped with rocking chairs, several upturned wooden nail kegs used for seats and supports for checker boards, and a pair of platform scales used to weigh freight and unpackaged merchandise sold by the pound. Women would share the front porch of the residence to visit with the merchant's wife exchanging recipes and talking women talk, while the children would play tag or hide-and-seek.

Young men would compete trying to see if any could straighten horse-shoes with their hands, or out lift each other by placing the weights on the balance beam of the scales, standing upon its plat-form, bending their knees, grasping the bottom of the scale's frame, and lifting upward attempting to make the balance beam travel to its highest limit. The most possible lift weight of that arrangement equaled the maximum weight for which the scales were designed. Horse-shoe games played along the edge of the dirt road near the front of the store often lasted until mid-night, the pegs illuminated by lantern light. Little boys and girls played marbles for keeps on the ground, each one usually carrying a sock full of marbles to and from the games.

No matter how many times I have entered a country store, an enchantment seemed to inhabit the place. Other than a rather dark interior, I always noticed wonderful odors, a mixture of spices, fruit, animal feed, fertilizer, dry-goods, leather, coffee, liniment, tobacco, and others too numerous to list. A rectangular room approximately fifty feet long and thirty feet wide with fifteen foot ceilings normally comprised the store. Show cases with wooden counter tops and glass fronts for displays of small merchandise extended almost the full length of the store on each side. A few open spaces between some, allowed to the merchant to pass behind the counters The counters were situated approximately four feet from each wall, providing room for the merchant to conduct business behind them the full length of the store.

As was true of the front porch, chairs and nail kegs were provided to make the winter-time and evening visitors feel welcome. Night-time illumination was provided by kerosene lamps suspended from the ceilings. Almost without exception, a barrel-shaped pot-bellied coal fired Burnside stove was positioned at the center of the store to provide winter heat. The exterior surface of those cast-iron stoves often became cherry red. A deep square pan or bucket containing ashes was always placed on the floor near the stove for the convenience of tobacco chewers and smokers into which to dispose of the by-products of their habits. Accurate aim and fantastic distances became almost an olympic art for some of those chewers.

Days were seldom lonely at a country store with the arrival of the mail carrier, people getting their mail, customers buying their needs, and salesmen representing wholesale suppliers. Farm customers usually relied upon the country merchant to order whatever they needed, because the merchants knew where to locate almost anything, he knew the salesmen, and he had the necessary money with which to make large purchases. Most freight orders and other supplies were delivered by railroad to a centrally located depot. Each merchant hired a neighbor who owned horses and a wagon to serve as his deliveryman. He would make trips to the depot, thus, making it unnecessary for the merchant to leave his store to re-supply his inventory.

It was amazing the number of items one could find at a country store. In simplest terms, one could find food, seeds, fertilizer, fencing, dish-ware, pots, pans, eating utensils, cloth, buttons, thread, needles, clothing, boots, shoes, medicine, kerosene, hardware, lamps, lanterns, flashlights, batteries, knives, clocks, cosmetics, tools, chain, horse harness, horseshoes, nails, lumber, furniture, baby chicks, and ducks. This list is by no means complete.

When automobiles began arriving in the countryside, most country merchants buried a steel tank at one corner of the front porch. A single hand-operated gasoline pump was mounted upon a corner of the front porch floor. A ten gallon glass cylinder with one gallon graduations etched into it was mounted atop the pump. There was only one grade of gasoline. Most customers served them selves by pumping the quantity of gas wanted. No electricity was involved. The customer stopped the pump where he wanted and simply allowed gravity to drain the gasoline into his car's fuel tank. To attest to the common honesty of country folk of that era, the customer would tell the merchant the amount of gasoline he had installed and the merchant accepted his word -- the way life should be. The earliest gasoline price I can remember was eighteen cents per gallon. Those were the closest resemblance to a service station to exist throughout many country miles for many years.

By year 1940, electric power lines began to reach remote country locations and automobiles also became commonplace. Along with electricity came refrigerators and all manner of electrical appliances. Within a few years, highway departments began paving farm to market roads, super-markets arrived in most small towns, so country people drove their cars past the country stores to reach the modern service stations, department stores, supermarkets, pharmacies, theaters, restaurants, hardware stores, and large clothing outlets. The ability to buy and preserve cold storage foods at home replaced the former supplies of the country store.

One by one, the country stores closed their doors and they became relics of bygone days. Now, many tourists who zoom down the highways at eighty miles per hour and who live in congested city environments feel a forlorn yearning for the simple slower pace of those early country 'Mayberry' days. Americans who have only heard older people such as I tell about those times, now search for a glimpse of that nostalgia. They revel at seeing what they think is an authentic old-time country store, but what they see is only a mirage. They rush from their multi-thousand dollar automobiles, pop coins into the nearest soft-drink machine located on the front porch, race Nike-clad feet inside the door, pop another coin into a compact disc player, and belly up to a lunch counter where they order a hamburger and fries. Some of the adults obtain a cup of coffee from an electric coffee maker and all agree that the place is really quaint. Even the adults may inquire why a ball of white twine is encased a small round metal cage dangling above a counter-mounted dispenser containing a large roll of brown butcher paper, or wonder what that hinge-jointed tobacco cutting knife was used for. They wonder why rows of shelves range from the floor to the ceiling on walls completely around the store and why a narrow ladder topped by a pair of minia-ture trolley wheels is attached to a monorail circling the entire store at ceiling height. Why is that old glass fronted cabinet full of spools of thread mounted upon wooden pegs? Why does that wooden barrel have a spigot and smells like vinegar? And why are men's boots with tops reaching knee height and women's shoes have buttons instead of laces on display? Should those bridles, saddles, and harness be hanging upon a rear wall in a place serving food? How can a horse wear a shoe? Why would a horse wear a collar? How come all of the women and girls in those old pictures are wearing floor-length dresses and bonnets? Why are all of the men and boys in the pictures wearing hats and ill-fitting suits that look like they need pressing? Why do you display all of those churns and crocks? And what were those large porcelain pots with lids and a bail used for? So goes millions of questions by those who will never know how it was. Also, many of those pretenders of whom the questions are asked do not know the answers.

A Perfect Example of a Perfect Example

An elderly lady named Nellie Dietz lived alone in a house at Rupert, West Virginia. Nellie was a lovely lady who looked and acted much younger than her silver gray hair would have lead you to believe. Her advanced years had not erased her beauty, her cheerful smile, nor dimmed the sparkle in her sky-blue eyes. There always seemed to be a well of unlimited energy that drove the body and spirit of that medium sized woman.

During the thirty years following the death of her husband, Nellie kept herself busy as a member of women's clubs and a local church. Through them, she developed lasting friendships. As many of her friends grew older, they became ill and disabled.

On or about the year 1985, the citizens of Rupert contributed money to buy a vacant store-building, which they developed into a community center. Near the same time, an organization called Meals On Wheels established a kitchen inside another vacant building for the purpose of providing hot meals and delivering them to elderly citizens too old and sick to cook for themselves.

Nellie discovered that living alone, very little time was needed to keep her own home neat and clean. With time to spare, she decided to dedicate the remainder of her life to helping other people who could not help themselves. She volunteered working shifts at Meals On Wheels and often delivering hot meals to old people who lived within walking distance of the kitchen. If help was needed for some activity at the Community Center, Nellie went there. If the local school, the churches, or the Fire Department needed help with fund raising events, Nellie volunteered. There were gaps between such projects, however, and Nellie did not feel that she was contributing all of the time that she could spend in service to others. She decided to continue doing all of those things, but when there was nothing else happening within the Community, she would work alone to help her friends.

Nellie began each day with a stroll through Rupert. An ordinary day for her consisted of visiting sick or shut-in friends. She often prepared breakfasts, went to the Post Office for them, delivered prescriptions from the drug store, did grocery shopping, and delivered the bags which were often quite heavy to their homes. She could always see what needed to be done. There may be dirty dishes to be washed, laundry to be done, a wood fire to be started, ashes to be carried out, wood or coal to be carried indoors, trash to be bagged and placed by the curb, letters to be written, another to be read, a phone call to be dialed for someone too blind to read the numbers, a newspaper to be read. Many people could not read or understand instructions written on a medicine bottle and many would forget the proper dosage. Nellie often arranged the daily doses of pills for a week inside specially designed boxes for that purpose.

Many old people are too weak to remove bottle caps or to open tightly sealed food packages. Some need help getting dressed or help getting in or out of a bath tub. Some need assistance walking to or from a car when visiting a doctor. It is nice to have someone waiting at home, when coming from a stay in a hospital. It is also comforting to have someone to sit and talk to after a dear friend or family member dies. Sometimes, it is nice to have someone just give you a warm friendly hug. Nellie did all of those things.

Nellie's good will crusade also included frequent visits to the local nursing home for sick people who could no longer live alone. She tried hard to let them know that they had not been forgotten. She also gladdened their lonely hearts by bringing a birthday card, a flower, a box of candy, and always s smile, a gentle touch, or a hug.

Two highways meet at the mid-section of Rupert. The town is three-quarters mile wide along one road and approximately two miles along the other. During the many years that Nellie was busy loving and caring for her neighbors during all extremes of weather, she must have walked a thousand miles inside the town limits.

As we all know, along with all of the happy days, sometimes there comes a sad day. Such a day came when Nellie, herself, became sick and had to have surgery. Months passed before she was strong enough to resume helping her less fortunate friends, but she kept in touch by telephone, until she was well enough to walk.

Her devotion to service has not gone unnoticed. On more than one occasion, the Mayor of Rupert accompanied by most of the town people have honored Nellie as a hero.

She died May 1, 1995 at the Washoe Progressive Care Center, Sparks, Nevada near Reno where she had gone to live with her daughter, Doris Hunter. She was much too modest to think of herself as a hero, but those who knew her are certain that she was much more. She was a National Treasure. Each of us has seen statues of bronze and stone to honor persons of note. Nellie's monument is etched in the loving memories of those whom she befriended. There is a line contained in a popular song which in essence states: 'It doesn't matter what you take with you , but what you leave behind when you go.'

It is appropriate that children as well as adults read this story, because it should be an inspiration to all. Any person would do well to live as unselfishly as Nellie did. The remarkable thing about the compassion she had for her neighbors was typical of most farm and small-town people who lived during the 'horse and buggy days' in America. No doubt, you have been told to 'love thy neighbor.' Perhaps Nellie was not much different than hundreds of people you have known, but she truly practiced the good life that her parents taught her was the way to live.

Each of us who listens to the News, knows that the way of life in America today is much different, but we should never forget the lessons exhibited by Nellie. That is, the most rewarding life is one in which we are of service to those less fortunate than ourselves. Those needing help are not hard to find. They are everywhere.

It is sad, but true. There are wonderful people who, through intelligence and hard work, create great things, while on the other hand, there are those who only destroy. Not everyone may have the time to devote your life on a daily basis such as Nellie did, but you can devote your life from this day forward to being a builder. You can start today building loyal friendships by doing a kind deed for your parents, another family member, a friend, a neighbor, or even a stranger. Do those things and you, too, may become like Nellie -- A Perfect Example of a Perfect Example.

A Place Called Weird

There was a time when the valley was a natural paradise. A clear stream of water with banks lined by ferns and a bed strewn with moss-covered rocks flowed to a distant river. It was also home to fish, frogs, lizards, and water insects. Tall grass and wild flowers grew inside natural clearings spreading from both sides of the stream, then rising to meet the massive forests of the high mountains extending many miles in all directions. The valley and forests were home to swarms of butterflies, bees, birds, and hordes of wild animals.

Thadeous Tittle and his pioneer family were the first non-Indian family to settle there and to claim as much free land as they wanted to serve their needs. Mr. Tittle was not greedy, so he cut enough chestnut trees to split into rails to enclose a small farm. He also cut enough hard-wood logs to build a dwelling house, cellar, wood shed, barn, grain bin, chicken house, and a pig sty. Without neighbors of course, initially there was no church, school, store, or Post Office.

The Tittles had loaded two large wagons with furniture, food, seeds, chickens, and two hogs and made the long journey from their former home in far-away Virginia. One wagon was pulled by a team of fine large horses; the other by a team of oxen. Behind one wagon, being led by a rope and halter, was a young red bull with a white face. Behind the other wagon, also being led by a rope, was the family milk cow.

Within several months, other pioneer families following the Tittle's wagon ruts arrived to also make the valley their homes. They, too, fenced claims to free land to create farms. As the community grew with more families arriving every few months, three roads were carved through the wilderness and intersected at one corner of Mr. Tittle's farm near his house.

Mr. Tittle saw the need for a country store and a Post Office, so he built a large store and also became the first Post Master of the village named Tittleville. Churches, a school, barbershop, and blacksmith shop were eventually built. Some people became harness-makers, shoe cobblers, quilt makers, weavers, tailors, etc.

A sad day came for Tittleville when mining engineers discovered vast amounts of coal deposited below the surface of the lovely mountains. With that discovery, the citizens of Tittleville had sudden dreams of growing rich.

Soon after the discovery of coal, executives of a large mining company informed the citizens that they had purchased all of the land and mineral rights of thousands of acres of mountain land surrounding and including the entire village of Tittleville. The Company installed a sawmill and began cutting the forest and sawing the lumber to build a new dwellings, a company store, cross-ties for a railroad, and heavy timbers for the construction of a coal tipple.

The beautiful hills were soon bare of trees; even millions of saplings were harvested to provide posts used to support the roof of the mine. Only scrub brush remained where the great forests once grew. The loggers damaged what once was the soft forest floor by creating deep ruts down the mountainsides as they dragged huge logs to the sawmill. Before long, heavy rains eroded the log ruts into deep ugly gullies. The topsoil thus washed away turning the beautiful stream into a brown muddy trench. The animals and birds moved away, because they no longer had a place to live.

Mr. Tittle had to close his store due to lack of business after arrival of the company store. It became clear that employees of the coal company were forbidden to make purchases anywhere other than the company store. Even Mr. Tittle's Post Office was taken away from him and was installed inside the new store. Only the community's name of Tittleville remained.

At the time Tittleville was first inhabited, very little United States money was seen or used. The nearest banks were hundreds of miles away. What was known as 'the barter system' had been used to provide pioneer families most of what they needed. This is how it worked: If a cobbler needed a pig, for example, he would trade a pair of shoes to a farmer who had pigs for which to trade. Another example may be that Mr. Tittle needed butter, eggs, cheese, and milk for sale at his store; he may trade some of each to a weaver for several yards of cloth. Now you understand that there may be thousands of examples. Once the cycle of trade began, it continued day after day throughout the community.

Once the coal company moved in, however, its employees became its slaves. The original settlers could not afford to hire lawyers to contest the coal company's claim that it now owned their farms. The company also advised them that it would closely surround their original houses with company houses and added a final contempt for the settlers by charging them rent for the houses which they, themselves, had built. The settlers were warned, either pay rent or move out. In order to remain, Mr. Tittle and his pioneer neighbors found it necessary to also become coal company employees.

Coal company employees were further enslaved, because they were never paid with real U.S. currency, but rather with 'play money' called 'scrip' coined and printed by the company, itself. Scrip could not be deposited at any bank other than by the company officers, nor could scrip from one company be spent at another mining company, who also created their own. Through the use of scrip, the company 'owned' every aspect of their employees' lives. Even the use of the 'barter' system was forbidden and would bring reprisal by the company's private police 'goons'. Every need had to be bought and paid for at the company store.

What was equally sad was that the men who dug the coal were required to load a minimum number of mine cars per day. If they failed for any reason, the mine Foreman would make a record of the failure and the miner would not be paid. Even on those days when a miner met his quota of loaded cars, the weigh-masters would report that the cars were partially loaded with slate or rock instead of clean coal. The weary miner's pay was reduced by the percentage the weigh-master declared. The store, on the other hand, could charge whatever they pleased for merchandise.

You may ask why didn't the miners simply ride the first coal train away from the area and never return? The reason they did not was because the company hired their own police force called 'railroad detectives.' Any caught attempting to leave by train or foot was brutally flogged and forced back to work. If one did succeed escaping, his family with all of their possessions was evicted from their house by the police. Friends and neighbors were forbidden to give them shelter and they were left to walk out of the area without food, money, or personal property. Life at Tittleville had grown very sad.

With the opening of the mine, hundreds of poor families arrived at Tittleville seeking a job and a place to live. The coal company anticipated their arrivals. The company hired throngs of carpenters to use lumber to build small cheap four-room houses on both sides of the roads, railroad, and the stream all the way up to the hollow where the mine was located. Every house, except the lavish ones for the mine executives, was monotonously alike with a black tar-paper roof, clap-board siding, double-hung wooden- sash windows, a small porch front and rear, a windowless front and back door, and a small red brick chimney located in the center of the roof. Each house was painted white with all window and door frames painted dark green. Each house was spaced six feet apart where possible.

Black dust from the coal tipple, smoke billowing from locomotives, the yellow sulfur-laden smoke from every chimney soon turned the houses a dirty depressing gray. Far from being least among the air pollutants, which on many days entirely blotted the sun from view, was the mountain of coal-waste slate dump, commonly called a 'gob pile', near the entrance to the mine. The sheer pressure of millions of tons of coal waste combined with pockets of oxygen ignited into a smoldering inferno. Once ignited by spontaneous combustion, it burned out of control resembling an aging volcano belching sulfurous smoke into the sky many years after the owners of the Tittleville coal mine took their profits and ran, leaving the community to die a slow ugly death.

At the time the Tittle family arrived in that once beautiful valley, the water in the stream was so nearly pure, one could drink it without worry. Before the first settlers had time to hand-dig their private wells, each family avoided polluting the stream as much as possible. As more people began to arrive, however, thoughtless people began using the stream for disposal of their household wastes. The instant result was that those who lived downstream began consuming the wastes of their upstream neighbors, resulting in out-breaks of fatal diseases, thus creating a cemetery atop a hill on Mr. Tittle's property.

As for the beautiful stream, its rapid, long, and torturous death had only begun. Especially after the arrival of the mining company, it became clogged by every imaginary kind of trash and waste. Since people no longer owned their homes, they took no pride in them. The coal company had made the lots so small, many people could easily stand upon their porches and throw trash either into the stream or the drainage ditches of the railroad and streets. What was equally bad, the mining company parked abandoned worn-out oil-leaking machinery along the stream and hollows leading to their mine. At the coal tipple and work areas just outside the mine, large amounts of waste grease and oil were deliberately poured upon the ground, often as a means of controlling dust. The waste oil also washed into the stream during storms.

The mine engineers knew that there was a major need for water at the mine as well as the need for water inside people's houses. As quickly as possible, earthen dams were constructed by damming some of the hollows above the town. Also, as entry tunnels were thrust deep into the mountains, huge pools of water were released. Rather than waste it, that water was also diverted behind the earthen dams to combine with rainfall and snow melt to form the town reservoir.

Mine water contained two major components, which, when exposed to oxygen in the atmosphere and sunlight began developing sulfuric acid from the sulfur and ferric acid from the iron content. Both were corrosive. Concentrated amounts of sulfuric acid can destroy human flesh and can eat through many of the hardest metals. Ferric acid causes metals to rust. Either or both acids diluted in drinking water over a prolonged period can encourage development of stomach ulcers and many other health problems involving kidneys, liver, intestines, and the circularly system. Combine all of that with the fact that lead pipes were used to form the water delivery system of Tittleville and the heavily polluted air that people breathed every day of the year was so injurious to their health, people, many of them young children, did not live very long.

Few if any creatures lived inside the reservoir due to the acidity of the water. Around its banks and along the drainage ditches where the combined acids seeped into the brown soil, great gobs of brilliant yellow ooze the consistency of thick paste much like that which Indians used to paint their faces before entering battle gave off a sickening putrid odor. The acids killed all aquatic stream life, vegetation, the moss, and turned the creek rock brown.

The days of the horse and wagon gradually became replaced by cars and trucks. Likewise, the old-fashioned ice box, wood-burning ranges, and oil lamps were replaced by refrigerators, electric ranges, and electric lights. The laundry tubs and washboards were discarded for washing machines Those new conveniences, however, created another kind of pollution which now joined all others as poor quality vehicles and appliances prematurely wore out or quit working. Once they became useless, they were similar to having a dead whale on hand. They had to be disposed of.

One day, Mr. Tittle died. His family buried him at the hilltop cemetery named in his honor. A monument in memory of Tittleville's most famous resident was erected at the head of his grave. Instead of honor and reverence, the town's trash mongers dealt him in death stunning disrespect by using the cemetery road to create a huge open-faced trash dump flush against the fence and the area surrounding his burial ground. The town's most famous citizen lay surrounded by junked cars, heaps of tires, washing machines, televisions, refrigerators, and anything else imaginable.

The day came when the last lump of coal had been mined. With suddenness, the mining company began removing its equipment, clearing the company store shelves of food and merchandise, locked all of the business buildings, and boarded the windows and doors. They simply abandoned their employees and left Tittleville a ghost town, except for the poor families who had no place else to go. Now Tittleville's greatest population consisted of dogs and cats whom their owners had abandoned.

Seemingly, to deal the once beautiful valley a final insult, strip mining companies came into the area and made the mountainsides hideous with raw high-walls of dirt, rocks, and mud. They completed their dirty-work quickly like thieves in the night, stealing the last vestige of Nature's former treasure. When they had removed the last speck of coal, they hastily moved out leaving the open wounds of their ugly destruction behind.

At the town limits of the three roads leading into Tittleville, signs with faded letters barely readable announces 'Welcome to Tittleville'. A few yards toward the town's interior are three more signs almost invisible among the brambles and piles of trash which admonish: 'Take Pride. Keep Tittleville Clean And Green'.

People hurrying past no longer honor Tittleville by its name; instead, they simply call it 'Weird'.

If by miracle, Nature would use its most gracious kindness and erase all of the evil that has been wreaked upon Mr. Tittle's valley, the lovely meadows, flowers, birds, bees, butterflies, and animals would return. The stream would sparkle again, the mountains would be green, and without man's ugly scars.

If on the other hand, instead of allowing water to flow down-hill as it naturally does, Nature would show its indignant wrath and unleash great floods of water flowing uphill through Tittleville Valley washing the town and all of its filth and trash to the tops of the mountains, Weird's greatest monument to its history with man would be the World's largest, ugliest, and most stinking trash dump.

Final thought: We are humans, not rats. We should not, therefore, live like rats. DO NOT LITER.

The Whisper

The elderly mountain climber parked his vehicle at a wide spot along the ancient log road at the foot of White Rock Mountain. It was the same spot where he had parked on each of his birthdays for the past several years. His objective this day, as always, was to climb to the summit of the rugged mountain to enjoy the view, to commune with Nature, and to meditate. That was a tradition, a ritual of sorts, which he had reserved for himself to enjoy alone.

After retiring from a working career, adding one year at a time eventually results in a rather high stack of birthdays. This one was number eighty three. Just as upon the occasion of all the others, he anticipated that the pleasure of the forthcoming climb would be familiar, difficult, but also a rewarding adventure. Life had been kind to him with a minimum of hard knocks along the way. He was content with his life, found each day exciting, and was thankful that Providence had given him excellent health and endurance.

After removing a small back-pack containing some food, water, a cell-phone, binoculars, matches, first aid supplies, and tissues, he locked his vehicle and began the steep assent of a small foot-hill via a seldom used electric power-line service road. The stinging chill of a swirling late November wind striking his face foretold the approaching winter. A deep layer of the forest's fallen leaves still bore the frost of the previous night, their dampness allowing his footsteps to fall almost silently upon the road. The wind, although not violent, continued to blow throughout the climb. It did not remain unpleasant as his exertion soon caused him to feel warm.

By the time he had reached the summit of the foot-hill, the frost had melted in the glow of the morning sun, which had risen above the horizon. At that point, the climber paused to eat a candy bar and to drink some water. The green valley, the villages and farms, the river, highways, surrounding mountains, and the blue autumn sky came into full focus as the bright sunlight aroused the landscape from its sleepy night. Aroma of newly fallen leaves permeated the forest air as the sounds of and unseen crows and blue jays drifted from shadowed ravines.

That location was actually the jumping-off point for the real climb to the mountain peak The hog-back ridge which the climber would use to reach his destination began rising immediately upon leaving the road. There was no path to follow along the relentless upward slope of constant forty-five degrees with a couple of short climbs of approximately sixty degrees. Forward progress to reach the summit was less than a mile, but footing was made difficult by the deep and slippery fallen leaves covering soft-ball sized round stones hidden from view. The height of the mountain is only approximately three thousand two hundred feet, but ascending that ridge was the actual challenge the old man had come to enjoy.

He did not regard White Rock Mountain as an adversary, but rather an old friend whom he had come to visit. He truly loved that mountain. From his home across a valley, he could observe it each day of the twenty-six years of residency there. He watched its magnificent transformation throughout the changing seasons. He saw it in times of brilliant sunshine, when shrouded by fog during summer rains, when it was clad in the verdant green of summer, its florescent autumn glory, or when cloaked by the deep snows of winter. He loved its silent beauty when bathed by moonlight and also on moonless nights when it appeared to be crowned by stars. The mountain seemed to possess a magnetism, which incessantly beckoned the climber to come near.

He made the climb steadied by a walking-stick with the carved face of a bearded man resembling the mythical Greek God Zeus. Progress was difficult, not so much because of the steep incline, but because of the hazardous footing upon the hard shale and rock strewn surface. Due to the infertility of the soil atop the spine-shaped ridge, vegetation consisted mostly of stunted oak, huckleberry , and broom-sage shrubs with shallow roots. They afforded little, if any, support, should the climber grasp them to prevent tumbling down the steep mountainside.

Slowly, carefully, deliberately the climber inched his way toward his goal. At two points a few hundred feet apart, rows of the white cliffs from which the mountain derived its name presented additional obstacles. Although neither were very high, they were coated by a type of white lichen upon their vertical surfaces, their upper surfaces were overhung by thick green moss, and water from recent rain seeped through their facial crevasses. Few shrubs or trees, which could afford hand-holds for a climber, penetrated them. It was with great caution that he negotiated passage over them. After one and one half hours, at times crawling upon 'all fours', the climber reached the summit.

The exhilaration upon reaching that enchanted spot was worth all of the effort he had expended. He felt as though he had arrived at the top of the world. He had previously climbed taller mountains in Germany and Switzerland, but none provided a more magnificent view or peaceful ambiance than the scene before him. What was more important to him, White Rock Mountain in West Virginia virtually stood in his front yard.

The neighboring mountains encircle White Rock in such a manner as to form lush narrow valleys, whose scalloped borders outlining the mouths of numerous deep hollows, each lined along two sides by ridges forming inverted Vs pinched together at their tops to form more mountain peaks. The valley leading from the base of White Rock along Howard's Creek extends eastward through Hart Run Village, past the Greenbrier Hotel's golf courses, then onward to White Sulphur Springs, West Virginia. From the climber's vantage point, the valley resembles a large salamander wiggling its progress along Howard's Creek past the many sand traps of the golf courses appearing to be white spots upon its bright green skin.

The mountains near and far, some with rounded summits, others with spines and peaks, all reflecting different hues of color depending upon their distant locations, caused the climber to imagine them as being huge pre-historic animals occupying a vast feed-lot. The landscape, dotted with alternating green farmland and forests extending for many miles in all directions, eventually blended with the horizon making it impossible to distinguish between earth and sky. The climber's senses became so absorbed by the wonderment of that almost magical experience, he felt as though he was entranced. He also became acutely aware that he was merely an insignificant speck inside that vast expanse.

He recalls that the wind began blowing the fallen leaves in little swirling eddies around his feet. He imagined them as being dancers pirouetting upon a stage. The sun had warmed the air and the climber began feeling drowsy. He sat upon a mound of dirt to rest before making his descent from the mountain, a task which would be almost as arduous as having climbed it. As he soon began to doze and dream, it was then that the wind seemed to carry an audible whisper to him.

A speaker seemed to say, "Rest here beside me for a while, my Friend. I have waited a long time for you to return to the mountain. You cannot see me, but I am the spirit of an ancient Indian buried beneath the mound upon which you are sitting. You are welcome here. Today, you are eighty three, but your great great great grand-father was a mere lad when I was buried here. I think that you love this spot as much as I always have since the days when I was a Seneca Indian youth. Many moons have passed since that time. You are now a child by comparison, but you are growing into the age of wisdom. Wisdom is often only the learning of simple truths. You must have noticed that my grave points East to West. It is symbolic in recognition that the sun, which regulates all things on this Earth, begins each day by rising in the East and closes each day by setting in the West. Between those two extremities, the wise man makes an honest endeavor to make life worthwhile for himself, to be a benefactor to others who desperately need help, and to try to bring to an end Man's cruelty to Man. Final wisdom has taught me that when man has viewed enough suns to fulfill his allotted time, he must surrender his space on Earth to make room for the newly born. It has always been true that, when an ancient one departs, a new child is born. Many people believe that the years which you have been counting were predicated upon the birth of a baby boy many centuries ago. I have spoken."

The climber awakened suddenly, pondering what he thought he had heard. When he stood to depart, he observed that the wind, which had been his sole companion throughout the day and had borne the admonition in the form of a whisper, was no longer blowing. Deeply moved by the experience, he reluctantly began the descent from the mountain.

In deep thought during his return to the foot of the mountain, he perceived the following lines:

WHITE ROCK MOUNTAIN

An Interstate Highway now passes his door
Where laurels and sycamores lined the glen before
White Rock Mountain, a mighty peak
His ancient feet bathed in Howard's Creek
Home of bass, red-eye, and trout
And chirping frog-lets when Spring breaks out
Sitting majestically upon his massive throne
Face bearded with oak and stately pine
Rills etched into his rugged steeps
A lap-robe of violets, dogwood, and rhododendron
Drapes his knees, the gales of winter gone
Grapevines into his vineyard creep
A faithful Sentinel, he stands always there
As Seasons come and Seasons go
Impervious to Winter's frigid air
Hoar frost white across his brow
No rushing streams, no nestlings now
His coat of snow the purest white
Silence his lone companion in the night
He yearns for lovely Greenbrier Mountain across the vale
The Love of his heart
She is so graceful and gay
Separated by the narrow valley at their feet
So near and yet so far away
Upon no force on Earth can they avail
Two Lovers who can never meet
Love notes the birds between the two exchange
Avowing faithfulness for all time
Blowing kisses upon the breeze
And praying for that Union so sublime
When Lovers can at last embrace
Forever face to face and their Love does not decline

CPSIA information can be obtained
at www.ICGtesting.com
Printed in the USA
FFOW01n1929171215
19595FF